HANDBOOK OF
20TH CENTURY OPERA

Da Capo Press Music Reprint Series

GENERAL EDITOR

FRANK D'ACCONE
University of California at Los Angeles

HANDBOOK OF
20TH CENTURY OPERA

(20TH CENTURY OPERA AT HOME & ABROAD)

by

May Silva Teasdale

DA CAPO PRESS • NEW YORK • 1976

Library of Congress Cataloging in Publication Data

Teasdale, May Silva.
  Handbook of 20th century opera - 20th century opera
at home & abroad.

  (Da Capo Press music reprint series)
  Reprint of the 1938 ed. published by E. P. Dutton,
New York.
  Includes indexes.
  1. Operas—Stories, plots, etc. 2. Opera—United
States. I. Title. II. Title: 20th century opera at
home & abroad.
ML1705.T26T9 1976   782.1'3   76-4920
ISBN 0-306-70783-7

162264

Published by Da Capo Press, Inc.
A Subsidiary of Plenum Publishing Corporation
227 West 17th Street, New York, N. Y. 10011

*XXTH CENTURY OPERA
AT HOME AND ABROAD*

MAY SILVA TEASDALE

20TH CENTURY

OPERA

AT HOME & ABROAD

1900 Through Season 1937-1938

NATIONALITY AND CHARACTER
TIME AND PLACE OF PREMIERES
ARRANGED CHRONOLOGICALLY

WITH PRINCIPALS OF CASTS IN THE

UNITED STATES

NEW YORK   E. P. DUTTON & COMPANY, INC.   1938

S. A. Jacobs, The Golden Eagle Press
Mount Vernon, N. Y.

To
MY DAUGHTER, MARGARET,
whose encouragement and aid
have ever been an inspiration

ACKNOWLEDGMENT

The following sources of assistance
are gratefully acknowledged:

Martens: *Book of Opera* (Fischer); Martens: *Thousand and One Nights of Opera* (Appleton); *Victor Book of Opera* (Victor Company); Bauer and Peyser: *Music Through the Ages* (Putnam); *Baker's Biographical Dictionary of Musicians* (Schirmer); Krehbiel: *Chapters of Opera* (Holt); New York *Times*; *Musical America*; Savannah (Ga.) Public Library; Secretary Metropolitan Opera Association, New York City.

April, 1938.   MAY SILVA TEASDALE
Savannah, Ga.

6

TABLE OF CONTENTS

¶ Opera is classified as Italian, French, American, etc. according to the language used by the author in his original libretto.

INDICES

OPERAS

Contents

INDEX I
LIST OF COMPOSERS
WITH PRONUNCIATION, DATES
AND PAGE REFERENCES

9

With Pronunciation, Dates

OF COMPOSERS
and Page References

11

With Pronunciation, Dates

OF COMPOSERS
and Page References

13

With Pronunciation, Dates

OF COMPOSERS
and Page References

KEY TO PRONUNCIATION

āle	ärm	câre	làst	măn
ēve	hĕr	mĕn	prėy	
īce	ĭs	polïce		
lôrd	mo͞on	nŏt	ōld	
menü	ūnit	ŭp	ûrn	

15

INDEX II

LIST OF OPERAS
WITH PAGE REFERENCES

With Page References

With Page References

OF OPERAS

With Page References

INDEX III

LIST OF OPERATIC STARS

WITH PAGE REFERENCES

23

With Page References

OF OPERATIC STARS
With Page References

25

With Page References

XXTH CENTURY OPERA
AT HOME AND ABROAD

ITALIAN OPERA

(PART I)

composed and produced

abroad, in the United States, or in both,

during the

XXth *Century*

1900 – Season 1937–1938

(inclusive)

Character of Italian Opera

Early Italian opera placed emphasis on the voice and vocal display. This standard ruled opera composers for many years, spreading into France, Germany, and England. But Christoph W. von Gluck, with the production of his *Orfeo ed Euridice*, began a drastic reform in Italian opera and thereby gained for himself the title, "The Father of Modern Opera."

31

Italian

La Tosca   Giacomo Puccini
                                               (1856-1924)
Première: Rome, 1900.
Première: New York, Metropolitan Opera House,
      1901, with Ternina as Tosca, Scotti as Scarpia,
      Cremonini as Cavaradosi.
Tragic opera in three acts. Text by Illica and Giacosa.
After Sardou's play.
Action: Rome, 1800.

   Tosca, a singer, is the mistress of Cavaradosi, a painter
who has aided in the escape of a political prisoner. Scarpia,
Chief of Police, desires Tosca for himself and tortures
Cavaradosi to make him reveal the whereabouts of his
friend. Tosca, hearing his groans, promises Scarpia she
will do as he wishes, be his, if he will sign an order for a
mock execution for Cavaradosi and a passport for the lovers. When he rises from his desk to claim her, she stabs
him and rushes to the cell of Cavaradosi, where she ex-
plains the plan. But Scarpia has played false. The bullets
were not removed, and Cavaradosi falls dead before the
firing squad. Tosca throws herself over the parapet and
is killed.

Zaza   Leoncavallo
                                               (1858-1919)
Première: Milan, Italy, 1900.
Première: San Francisco, 1903.
Première: New York, Metropolitan Opera House,
      1920, with Farrar as Zaza, Crimi as Dufresne,
      Amato as Cascart, the manager of Zaza.

32

AT HOME AND ABROAD

Italian

Lyric drama in four acts. Text by composer.
Story after a play by Simon and Berton—a posthumous
work.
Action: Paris at the beginning of the twentieth century.

Zaza, a cabaret dancer, wins a wager that she can make
Dufresne fall in love with her, but herself falls in love
with him. Her manager, to get her back to the theatre,
tells her that Dufresne spends much time with a woman
in Paris. Zaza discovers that this is his wife and sends him
back to his family.

Excerpts from this opera were given at the composer's
concerts in 1906 when he visited America.

Farrar made her farewell operatic appearance as Zaza
at the Metropolitan in 1922.

Adrienne Lecouvreur   Francesco Cilea
                                           (1866-   )

Première: Milan, 1902. Caruso created the title role
Maurice.
Première: New York, Metropolitan Opera House,
1907, with Lina Cavalieri as Adrienne, Caruso as
Maurice, Journet as the Prince, Jacoby as the
Princess, Scotti as Michonnet, stage manager of
the Comedie Francaise.
Tragic opera in four acts.
Book after Scribe's play.
Action: Paris, 1730.

33

Italian

Adrienne, an actress, gives a bunch of violets to an un-known officer in the foyer of the theatre. She is on her way to a supper at the villa of the Prince, where she is to meet Count Maurice de Saxe. There she finds that the Count is her unknown admirer to whom she had given the violets and that the Princess is her rival. She wins a verbal and vocal contest with the Princess and leaves in triumph. She pawns her jewels to help Maurice make himself a Duke. At her lodgings she receives a casket containing the bunch of faded violets. Thinking her lover has sent them to show his love she inhales their perfume. The Princess has sent them and has steeped them in poison. When Maurice comes to ask Adrienne to marry him she dies in his arms.

Germania   Alberto Franchetti
                                                    (1860-   )

Première: Milan, 1902.
Première: New York, Metropolitan Opera House,
         1910, with Toscanini conducting, and Emmy
         Destinn as Ricke, Caruso as Loewe, Amato as
         Worms.
Historical music drama in three acts, with prologue
     and epilogue.
Book by Illica.
Action: Napoleonic Germany.

Worms seduces Ricke, the wife of his friend Loewe. When Loewe finds it out later, his wife, who really loves her husband, flees. A duel between seducer and husband is stopped by the Queen who pleads for their swords for their country first. Worms dies on the battlefield and Loewe with his dying breath forgives.

Siberia   Giordano
                                                     (1867-   )
Première: Milan, 1903.
Première: New York, Metropolitan Opera House,
        1908, with Agostinelli as Stephana, Zenatello as
        Vassili, Casauron as the Prince, Sammarco as
        Gleby, the Prince's spy.
Tragic opera in three acts.
A tale of crime and retribution. Libretto by Illica.
Action: Czarist Russia.

Stephana, mistress of the Prince, falls in love with Sergeant Vassili who believes her pure. When he finds his mistake he wounds the Prince and is exiled to Siberia. Stephana, purified by her love, obtains permission to join him. She exposes the man who had caused her downfall and he in turn betrays her to the authorities. Stephana is shot while trying to escape with Vassili and dies in his arms.

Inquisitive Women (Le Donne Curiose)   Wolf-Ferrari
                                                     (1876-   )
Première: Munich, 1903.

35

Italian

Première: New York, Metropolitan Opera House,
1912, with Toscanini conducting, and Farrar as
Rosaura, Bella Alten as Columbina, Jadlowker as
Florindo, Scotti as Lelio.
Lyric comedy in three acts.
Libretto by Sugana, after Goldini.
Action: Venice, middle of eighteenth century.

The wives and sweethearts of the members of a certain
club are curious to know what goes on there, being sure
there must be "carryings on." They beg in vain to be admitted. One of them, Rosaura, coaxes her lover's key and
the password. They enter secretly and find the men—eat-
ing a good dinner! They are invited to join the men and
enjoy the dinner with them. Later they dance, and all ends
merrily.

Resurrection	Franco Alfano
	(1876-)

Première: Turin, 1904.
Première: Chicago, 1926 (American première), with
Mary Garden as Katuscha, Fernand Ansseau as
Prince Dimitri, Georges Baklanoff as Simonson.
Music drama in four acts. Libretto by C. Hanau.
Story after Tolstoi's novel, greatly condensed.
Action: Russia, nineteenth century.

Katuscha is betrayed by Prince Dimitri. She sees him
board a train with a woman companion and her hopes
vanish. Years later she is convicted of murder. Dimitri

visits her in prison. He is repentant and offers to marry her. She refuses and he follows her into exile. She is pardoned, still loving Dimitri, but she refuses to marry him. She finally marries Simonson, one of her fellow prisoners, and goes to Siberia with him.

Madame Butterfly   Puccini
                                                      (1858-1924)

Première: Milan, 1904.
Première: Washington, D.C., 1906.
Première: New York, Savage Opera Co., 1906.
        (Garden Theatre)
Première: Metropolitan Opera House, 1907, with
        Farrar as Cho-Cho-San, (Madame Butterfly),
        Caruso as Pinkerton, Homer as Suzuki, Scotti
        as Sharpless, the U.S. Consul.
Japanese lyric tragedy in three acts. Text by Illica
        and Giacosa.
After the story by John Luther Long.
Action: Nagasaki, Japan, beginning of twentieth century.

Lieut. B. F. Pinkerton of the U. S. Navy marries Cho-Cho-San (afterwards known as Madame Butterfly) according to Japanese law. When his vessel is ordered away he promises to return "when the robins nest again." Three years pass and Butterfly faithfully watches for his return. When his ship is finally sighted in the harbor she decorates the little house with flowers and she and her little son, Trouble, with Suzuki the maid, watch all night for his return. When he arrives in the morning it is with his American wife who offers to adopt the baby and bring

37

him up as her own if Butterfly will give him up. Butterfly tells Pinkerton to return later for the child and when he does he finds Butterfly dying beside the baby whose eyes are blindfolded and in whose hand is an American flag. Butterfly has killed herself with her father's sword of honor on which is engraved "To die with honor when one can no longer live with honor."

L'Oracolo   Franco Leoni
                                                   (1864-   )
Première: London, 1905.
Première: New York, Metropolitan Opera House,
        1915, with Scotti as Chim-Fen and Bori as Ah-Joe.
Tragic opera in one act. Text by Zanoni.
After Fernald's play. *The Cat and the Cherub.*
Action: Chinese Quarter of San Francisco just before
        the great fire of 1906.

Ah-Joe, beautiful niece of Hu-Tsin, is in love with San-Lui and has refused the advances of Chim-Fen, keeper of an opium dive. Chim-Fen in revenge steals the infant son of Hu-Tsin, who announces that whoever rescues the child will receive the hand of Ah-Joe as a reward. San-Lui enters the cellar of Chim-Fen and is ascending the steps with the child when he is killed by Chim-Fen who disappears with the child. Ah-Joe goes mad when she sees the dead San-Lui. His death is avenged by his father who finds Chim-Fen, rescues the child and kills the wicked Chim-Fen.

Scotti made his last appearance on the opera stage as "Chim-Fen" in 1933.

AT HOME AND ABROAD

Italian

Secret of Susanne   Wolf-Ferrari
                                                      (1876-   )

Première: Munich, 1909.
Première: New York, Metropolitan Opera House,
      1911, by the Philadelphia-Chicago Co., with Caro-
      lina White as Susanne, Mario Sammarco as the
      Count, Francesca Daddi as Sante.
Lyric drama in one act. Text by Kalbeck.
Story from the French of Golisciani.
Action: A drawing-room in Piedmont, 1840.

Susanne, lovely wife of Count Gil, secretly smokes. The
Count, always smelling the odor in her boudoir, thinks
she has a lover. Thinking to surprise them, he comes in
unannounced and finds her alone—smoking!

Girl of the Golden West   Puccini
                                                      (1858-1924)

World Première: New York, Metropolitan Opera
      House, 1910, with Destinn as Minnie, Caruso as
      Dick Johnson, Amato as Jack Rance. Toscanini
      conducted.
Tragi-romantic opera in three acts. Text by Zangarini
      and Civinini.
Story based on a tale by Bret Harte.
Action: California in the days of the gold rush, 1849.

Minnie, keeper and owner of the Polka Dot Saloon

39

Italian

meets Dick Johnson, an outlaw, who, as the Mexican bandit Ramerrez, robs stage-coaches and terrorizes the community. Captivated by the evident innocence and purity of Minnie he abandons his plan to rob her safe and falls in love with her instead. Wounded by a pursuing posse headed by Rance the sheriff, he finds his way to the cabin of Minnie who hides him. His presence in the cabin is betrayed by blood dripping from the rafters of the garret where he is hidden. Minnie challenges Rance to a poker game. If she wins, Dick goes free. If she loses, she will marry Rance. She wins, by cheating. As Dick tries to escape from the cabin he is caught and is about to be lynched when Minnie arrives and her pleas win his freedom. They are allowed to leave together to begin life anew in some other place.

Isabeau   Mascagni
                                                        (1863-   )

Première: Buenos Aires, 1911.
Première: Chicago, 1917, by Chicago Opera Co., with
    Rosa Raisa as Isabeau, Guilo Crimi as Folco, Giacomo Rimini as King Raimondo.
Première: New York, 1918, by the same company at
    the Lexington Theatre.
Legendary tragic opera.
Story based on the legend of Lady Godiva who, renamed Isabeau, is in this case the King's chaste
    daughter instead of his wife as in the legend.
Action: England, 1040.

Refusing obedience to her father, King Raimondo, in the matter of the choice of a husband, Isabeau is made to ride through the city naked. Folco, a pure-minded youth is shocked at the evil thoughts expressed about the lovely girl and showers her with flowers as she passes. Escaping the vulgar mob he is imprisoned under a death sentence though he declares himself innocent of any wrong. Isabeau believes him and hastens to her father to tell him of their love. Folco is murdered by the mob and Isabeau kills herself.

Conchita   Riccardo Zandonai
                               (1883-   )

Première: Milan, 1911.
Première: New York, Metropolitan Opera House, 1913, by Chicago-Philadelphia Opera Co., with Tarquini as Conchita, Dalmores as Matteo.
Romantic opera in three acts. Text by Vaucaire and Zandonai.
Story founded on Pierre Louys' *The Woman and the Puppet*.
Action: Seville, Spain, early twentieth century.

Conchita, a cigar-worker, runs away from rich Matteo who tries to force his attentions on her. When he finds her she is a dancer in a low dancehall. He persuades her to live in a little house he has prepared for her. She refuses him admittance at midnight, pretending she has a lover hidden. Not until he gives her a good beating does she confess that she loves him, and all is well.

41

XXth CENTURY OPERA

Italian

===

Jewels of the Madonna	Wolf-Ferrari
	(1876-)

Première: Berlin, 1911.
Première: Chicago, 1912, (American Première)
    Chicago Grand Opera Company, with Carolina
    White as Maliella, Amadeo Bassi as Gennaro,
    Mario Sammarco as Rafaele.
Première: New York, Metropolitan Opera House,
    (first time) 1912, with same company.
Tragic opera in three acts, two intermezzi. Text by
    Zangarini and Golisciani.
Action: Naples. Early twentieth century.

The plot is a melodramatic picture of the colorful Neapolitan life. Maliella who has been taken from the streets by a foster-mother, longs for the gayety of the life which she has left. Her foster-brother Gennaro, a blacksmith, is in love with her, but she flirts with Rafaele, a gangster leader. She is about to run away with Rafaele but Gennaro prevents her. He hears her dare Rafaele to steal the jewels of the Madonna, and determines to do so himself. When he brings them to her Maliella yields to him. She goes to the meeting place of Rafaele and his gang, and when Rafaele learns that she has already given herself to Gennaro he throws her on the floor. Her shawl thrown aside, the jewels are revealed. The superstitious crowd flee and when Gennaro enters, Maliella casts the jewels at his feet and rushes out to throw herself into the sea. Gennaro stabs himself before the image of the Virgin on the wall.

42

L'Amore Medici (Dr. Cupid)   Wolf-Ferrari
                                      (1876-   )
Première: Dresden, 1913.
Première: New York, Metropolitan Opera House,
    1914, with Lucrezia Bori as Lucinda, Pini-Corsi as
    Arnolfo her father, Itallo Cristalli as Clitandro, a
    young doctor. Toscanini conducted.
Lyric comedy. Text by Golischiani.
Story after Moliere's comedy transferred to an Italian
    rococo setting.
Action: Vicinity of Paris, reign of Louis XIV, about
    1665.

   Lucinda's lover, Clitandro, a young doctor, is promised
her hand if he can cure her illness. Knowing exactly what
is the matter with her heart, he cures her and so gains her
for his wife.

Love of the Three Kings   Italo Montemezzi
   (Amore dei tre re L')   (1875-   )
Première: Milan, 1913.

Première: New York, Metropolitan Opera House,
    1914, with Bori as Fiora, Ferrari-Fontana as Avito,
    Didur as Archibaldo. Toscanini conducted.
Tragic opera in three acts.
Text by Bennetti from his book of the same title.
Action: A remote section of Italy in the tenth century.

43

Italian

Blind old King Archibaldo is suspicious of his daughter-in-law, Fiora, wife of his absent son, Manfredo. Circumstances make him believe she has a lover although he cannot discover his identity. To avenge his son's honor he strangles Fiora. Manfredo, returning, is heartbroken. The old King smears the lips of the dead girl with a poison in order to catch the supposed lover. An old suitor, Avito, slips into the death chamber and kisses the lips which have been denied him in life. He falls dead, warning Manfredo, who has entered, not to kiss his wife. Manfredo sinks beside the bier and kisses her. Old Archibaldo, coming in to discover who has been caught in his trap, finds Avito and his son dead beside the bier of Fiora.

NOTE: Edward Johnson made his Metropolitan debut as Avito in 1922.

Francesca da Rimini   Zandonai
                                        (1883-   )

Première: Turin, 1914.
Première: New York, Metropolitan Opera House,
          1916, with Alda as Francesca, Martinelli as Paolo,
          Amato as Gianciotto.
Tragic opera in five acts. Text by Tito Riccordi.
Story based on an old medieval tragedy of Dante's time.
Action: Ravenna and Rimini, Italy, thirteenth century.

Gianciotto, ugly and deformed, has won the lovely Francesca for his wife and sends his young brother Paolo to marry her as his proxy and bring her to him. Paolo and Francesca fall in love. Another brother, Malestino, offers to poison Gianciotto (knowing that Francesca hates and fears her husband) if Francesca will be his. She refuses. Malestino hints to Gianciotto of wrong between Paolo and Francesca. In Gianciotto's absence the lovers are together. He returns suddenly and is about to kill Paolo with his sword when Francesca rushes between them and receives the death wound. Gianciotto then kills Paolo.

Madame Sans-Gene   Umberto Giordano
                                                    (1867-   )
Première: New York, Metropolitan Opera House,
        1915, with Farrar as Mme. Sans-Gene, Martinelli
        as Lefebvre, Amato as Napoleon, Althouse as de
        Neipperg. Toscanini conducted.
Comedy opera in four acts.
Story after play by Sardou and Moreau. Text by
        Simone.
Action: Paris, 1792, 1811.

Madame Sans-Gene, a laundress, hides de Neipperg, an Austrian officer pursued by the Revolutionary mob. Her jealous lover, Sergeant Lefebvre, is much relieved when he finds not a lover but a wounded enemy groaning on her bed. Years later when the Empire is in its glory, Napoleon insists that Lefebvre, now Duke of Dantzig and Marshal, divorce his wife because her free and easy manners offend the court, upset all rules of etiquette, etc. She is ordered to appear before Napoleon. She wins him to forgiveness and favor by showing him an unpaid laundry bill made when he was a poor lieutenant of artillery. She saves the situation later when she proves the innocence

Italian

of his Empress, Marie-Louise when Napoleon suspects her of intrigue with Count de Neipperg. Napoleon tells Lefebvre that he should thank heaven for such a wife as Sans-Gene.

Lodoletta   Mascagni
                                               (1863-   )

Première: Rome, 1917.
Première: New York, Metropolitan Opera House,
    1918, with Farrar as Lodoletta, Caruso as
    Flammeau.
Tragic opera in three acts.
Story after Ouida's *Two Little Wooden Shoes.*
Action: Holland and Paris. Middle nineteenth century.

Flammeau, an artist from gay Paris, wins the love of Lodoletta, a village maiden and then casts her away. She walks to Paris and dies in the snow under the window of her lover, who weeps and curses himself over her corpse.

La Rondine   Puccini
(The Swallow)   (1858-1924)

Première: Monte Carlo, 1917.
Première: New York, Metropolitan Opera House,
    1928, with Bori as Magda, Gigli as Alfred.
Lyric comedy in three acts.

46

AT HOME AND ABROAD
Italian

Text by Adami.
Action: Paris and Nice. Middle of nineteenth century.

Magda, mistress of a rich banker, Rambaldo, falls in love with Alfred, son of an old friend of the banker. She deserts Rambaldo and with Alfred goes to Nice. Alfred writes his parents of his love. They reply that if she is a good girl and virtuous all will be well. Magda, feeling unworthy and unwilling to spoil her lover's life, returns to Rambaldo.

Puccini's Trittico

(1) *Gianni Schicchi*   Puccini
                                       (1858-1924)

Première: New York, Metropolitan Opera House, 1918, with Easton as Schicchi's daughter, Lauretta, Crimi as her lover, Rinnucio, de Luca as Schicchi, Didur as Simone.
Humorous opera in one act. Text by Forgano.

Donati has died leaving all his wealth to charity. The neighbor, Gianni Schicchi, pretending to the relatives to aid them in getting all the money, with their consent, gets into Donati's bed, impersonates the "dying" man, sends for a lawyer, has a new will made which he signs, leaving everything—to himself, Schicchi!

47

Italian

(2) *Il Tabarro*   Puccini
     (The Cloak)   (1858-1924)

Première: New York, Metropolitan Opera House,
    1918, with Claudia Muzio as Giorgetta, Crimi
    as Luigi, Montesanto as Michele.
Tragic opera in one act. Text by Adami.
Story after Didier Gold's *La Hauppelande*.
Action: Michele's barge on the river Seine, nine-
    teenth century.

Luigi, a longshoreman, is the lover of Giorgetta, wife
of his fellow-worker, Michele. Luigi tells Giorgetta to
strike a match when it is safe for him to come aboard.
Michele comes. Giorgetta says she is tired and goes down
to the cabin. Michele strikes a match to light his pipe.
Luigi climbs aboard. Michele strangles him and covers up
the body with his coat. He continues smoking. Giorgetta
has heard a fall and comes up fearfully. Michele tears the
coat aside and throws her on the corpse.

(3) *Sister Angelica*   Puccini
                                            (1858-1924)

Première: New York, Metropolitan Opera House,
    1918, with Farrar as Sister Angelica, Flora
    Perini as her heartless aunt, the Princess.
Tragi-sentimental opera in one act.
Action: An Italian convent, seventeenth century.

Angelica has been betrayed and becomes a nun. She begs her aunt to tell her of her nameless child. The aunt sternly replies that it is dead. Angelica kills herself, praying forgiveness. Angels appear and take her to heaven.

La Nave   *Montemezzi*
(The Ship)   (1875-   )

Première: Milan, 1918.
Première: Chicago, 1919, Chicago Opera Association, with Rosa Raisa as Basiliola, Alessandro Dolci as Marco, Giacomo Rimini as Sergio. Composer conducted.
Tragic symbolic opera with prologue and three acts.
Story based on D'Annunzio's drama.
Action: Venice, eighth century.

The four brothers of Basiliola Falcedo have had their eyes put out by rival politicians, Marco and Sergio. Basiliola captivates them in a wanton dance. Marco is made jealous of his brother and kills him for her sake. His crime cools his passion and he orders Basiliola nailed to the prow of the great war ship of Venice as it goes to battle.

Edipo Re   Leoncavallo
(King Œdipus)   (1858-1919)

Première: Chicago, 1920, with Dorothy Francis as Gioasta the Queen, Titta Ruffo as King Œdipus.
Première: New York, Metropolitan Opera House, 1921, with Chicago Opera Association.

49

Mythological opera in one act. The composer reduced the five acts of the drama to one act. He died before the score was finished.

King Œdipus marries Gioasta, Queen of the Thebans. When a seer reveals the fact that Gioasta is the mother of Œdipus, the Queen kills herself and Œdipus tears out his eyes and wanders about the earth in misery until he finally dies.

Anima Allegra	Franco Vittadini
(The Joyous Soul)	(1884-)

Première: Rome, 1921.
Première: New York, Metropolitan Opera House,
    1923, with Bori as Consuelo, Kathleen Howard as
    Donna Sacramento, Lauri-Volpi as Don Pedro.
Romantic opera in three acts. Text by Adami.
Story after the Fratelli Quintero comedy, *Elgenic Alegre*.
Action: Andalusia, 1830.

Donna Sacramento lives a gloomy, isolated life on her country estate in Andalusia. Her son, Don Pedro, spends a gay life in Granada and is seldom at home. Consuelo, the niece of Donna Sacramento, comes for a visit. She is full of life, wears lovely clothes and makes the place ring with gayety and laughter. Don Pedro comes home and remains. The outcome is marriage with the beautiful Consuelo.

50

Piccolo Marat	Mascagni
	(1863-)

Première: Rome, 1921.
Melodramatic opera in three acts. Text by Forzano.
The story is a dramatization of the days of the French
    Terrorist, Jean Baptiste Carrier.
Action: Nantes, time of French Revolution.

The production of this opera "was the occasion of a
demonstration such as has seldom been given any opera
before. The composer, who conducted the performance,
was compelled to respond to over forty curtain calls."
                  (Musical America, June 4, 1921.)

A French nobleman comes to Nantes secretly, to rescue
his mother from prison. Outwardly he is a blood-thirsty
Terrorist and makes friends with the chief, Orso, in whose
home he meets Maliella, Orso's niece, a pure and lovely
girl. They fall in love and Little Marat, as he has been
nicknamed by the Terrorists, with the aid of Maliella and
a ship-carpenter, rescues his mother from the prison and
all escape.

Deborah e Jaele	Ildebrando Pizzetti
	(1880-)

Première: Milan, 1922.
Première: Rome, 1932.
Biblical tragic opera in three acts. Drama of high moral
    conception and of soul conflicts.
Awarded National Prize in 1931 — 50,000 lire.

51

162264

Italian

The Canaanites have trespassed upon the possessions of the Jews. Deborah, the prophetess demands war. The beautiful Jaele plans to deceive and win Sisera, King of the Canaanites, but falls in love with him and he with her. Their love is hopeless, for she must be true to her country. Rather than have Sisera fall into the hands of the Jews, she invites him to her tent, gives him food and drink and while he sleeps, kills him.

La Cena Delle Beffe	Giordano
(Supper of the Jesters)	(1867-)

Première: Milan, 1924.
Première: New York, Metropolitan Opera House,
    1926, with Alda as Ginevre, Gigli as Giannetto,
    Ruffo as Neri.
Melodramatic opera in four acts.
Story based on Sam Benelli's play of the same title.
Action: Florence. Time of Lorenzo il Magnifico.

Giannetto, a Florentine poet, has been made the butt of many pranks by Neri and Gabriello, whom he hates. Upon finding that his sweetheart, Ginevra, has been forced to become the mistress of Neri, Giannetto vows vengeance and swears that he himself will do some "jesting." At a gay supper, Giannetto makes Neri drunk, steals his key, leaving him bound in the wineshop, and goes to Ginevra's room. Neri frees himself and finds Giannetto locked with Ginevra in her room. The next night Neri watches and when Giannetto comes from Ginevra's room, stabs him, only to find that he has killed his own brother whom the clever Giannetto has admitted to Ginevra's room in his place that night.

Turandot (The Chinese Princess)	Puccini (1858-1924)

Première: Milan, 1926.

Première: New York, Metropolitan Opera House, 1926, with Jeritza as the Princess, Max Altglass as the Emperor Altoum, Lauri-Volpi as Prince Calaf the unknown.

Fairy opera in three acts. Text by Simon and Adam.

Story based on Gozzi's fairy play (after an Eastern legend).

Action: Pekin, China. Legendary times.

The Princess Turandot demands all suitors to answer three questions. If they cannot, they are put to death. Calaf, an exiled Prince, guesses the answers but Turandot would rather die than marry him. He tells her he will give her up if she can tell him the name of the King's son (himself) who became a beggar and was most fortunate (guessing her riddles) when fortune favored him least. Turandot learns who he is, and when the marriage service begins, she calls his name and tells him to seek another wife. The Prince tries to stab himself but she stays the dagger, because she loves him.

NOTE: This is a posthumous opera, being completed by F. Alfano.

53

Italian

Madame Imperia   Franco Alfano
                                       (1876-   )

Première: Turin, 1927.
Première: New York, Metropolitan Opera House,
     1928, with Maria Müller as Madame Imperia,
     Philine Falco as Balda, Frederick Jagel as Filippo
     Mala, Pinza as the Chancellor.
Humorous opera in one act.
Plot derived from one of Balzac's *Contes Drolatiques.*
Action: France, 414 A. D.

   Madame Imperia, a lovely courtesan, has three suitors
for her favors—a Chancellor, a Prince and a lowly clerk.
The clerk, because of his audacity, wins her.

La Campana Sommersa   Ottorino Respighi
   (The Sunken Bell)   (1879-1936)

Première: Hamburg, Germany, 1927.
Première: New York, Metropolitan Opera House,
     1928, with Elizabeth Rethberg as Rautendelein
     the Fairy, Martinelli as Heinrich, Nanette Guil-
     ford as Magda, Enzio Pinza as the Pastor.
Allegorical opera in four acts. Text by Guastalla.
     Founded on Gerhart Hauptman's drama of the
     same title.

   Heinrich, the bellcaster, dreams of a master bell ringing from the top of the mountain. He casts such a bell and
places it there, but it disturbs the people of the upper

54

world and they send it crashing down from the mountain into the lake below. Heinrich is heartbroken. He meets a fairy as he wanders in the woods. She sees that his pagan soul must be aroused. His wife, Magda, dies and the Pastor tells him that sin and heresy are working in him. Heinrich cries: "If this be so may the sunken bell toll again." He sees the phantoms of his children bearing an urn filled with Magda's tears. The bell tolls by the hand of his gentle wife, Magda, who lies at the bottom of the lake.

Fra Gherado   Pizzetti
                                       (1800-   )

Première: Milan, 1928.
Première: New York, Metropolitan Opera House,
       1929, with Edward Johnson in the title role and
       Maria Müller as Mariola.
Tragic opera in three acts.
Action: Parma, 1260. Time of the Crusades.

   Fra Gherado, a weaver of Parma, sells his possessions and gives all to the poor. Mariola, a young girl who lives near by with a wicked aunt, begs his protection. They fall in love, but Gherado conceives the idea that Mariola is of the devil and drives her out. She is waylaid by two drunken sailors and Gherado rescues her. The next morning Gherado, again convinced of sin, sends her away forever. He becomes the head of a religious order, inwardly despising himself. Miracles are ascribed to him but he disclaims all. A mother brings her dying child for his prayers. He refuses and she curses him. Mariola comes out of the crowd to comfort him. She has borne him a son which

55

Italian

has died. Gherado is filled with remorse and begs her to go away with him. She pleads with him to remain true to his vows. He is arrested and a woman whose child has been killed in one of the riots following his arrest stabs Mariola to death, while Gherado is led out to be burned at the stake.

NOTE: Pizzetti's music is in keeping with the period of liturgic and Gregorian styles.

Notte di Zoraima Montemezzi
(Zoraima's Night) (1875-   )

Première: Milan, 1930.
Première: New York, Metropolitan Opera House,
    1931, with Rosa Ponselle as the Princess, Jagel as
    Muscar, Mario Basiola as Pedrito.
Tragic opera in one act. Text by Mario Ghisalberti.
    An Inca theme, an episode of the troublesome
    times between the Spanish followers of Pedrito
    and the Inca insurgents.
Action: West Coast of South America,
    sixteenth century.

Princess Zoraima has a princely lover, Muscar. He has planned to overcome the Spaniards in their invasion of Peru, but the plan fails and he is wounded. He hides near the palace of Zoraima. Pedrito, commander of the Spaniards, is in love with Zoraima and is torn between his love and his duty, as his followers wish to kill Zoraima and

56

Muscar. Zoraima requests the Spaniards to allow Pedrito to come to her and they consent. She promises to give herself to him in exchange for the life of Muscar. When Muscar has been conducted to safety she plunges a dagger into her breast to escape the Spaniard, Pedrito.

La Vedova Scaltra   Wolf-Ferrari
                                        (1876-   )

Première: Berlin, 1931.
Comic opera in three acts. Text by Goldoni. A delightful satire, translated into German by Dahms.

Vedova Scaltra is a gay widow. She has four suitors—a slow-moving Englishman, an arrogant Spaniard, a bubbling Frenchman and an Italian lackey. The final triumph of birth over gold, glory and grace ends a clever satire.

La Donna Serpente   Alfredo Casella
                                        (1883-   )

Première: Rome, 1932.
Première: Mannheim, Germany, 1934.
Fantastic comedy opera in three acts. Text by Lodovici.
Story based on Gozzi's fairy tale.

King Altidor is compelled to undergo cruel tortures and difficult labors in order to win back to mortal shape his wife Miranda, daughter of the King of the Fairies. She has been turned into a serpent by her husband's curse because she would not answer his questions as to her real identity. This curse he must redeem by his own suffering, and he finally wins her back.

NOTE: The production was cordially received. The composer conducted. This was his first opera.

Marie Egiziaca   Respighi
(The Egyptian Mary)   (1879-1936)

Première: New York, Carnegie Hall, 1932, with Charlotte Boerner in title rôle, Nelson Eddy as the Abbot Zosimo, and the Pilgrim.
A mystery music drama in three episodes:
    1 – Port of Alexandria, Egypt.
    2 – The Temple in Jerusalem.
    3 – In the Desert.

Marie Egiziaca, at the Port of Alexandria, begs a sailor to let her go on a voyage in his ship and offers herself as payment. The sailor is warned by a stranger, but takes her with him. She wanders to Jerusalem and tries to go into the temple but is not allowed to enter the sacred portals. In the third episode Mary, now an old woman, wanders in a desert. She seeks the Abbot Zosimo, begs his blessing, and dies.

La Farsa Amorosa   Zandonai
(Three-cornered Hat)   (1883-   )

Première: Rome, 1933.

58

Comic opera in three acts, five scenes, and two comic
  interludes.
Plot after D'Alarcon's story, *The Three-Cornered
  Hat*.
Action: Lombardy, 1600.

Don Eugenio Zeniga, wearer of the official three-
cornered hat, is upset from a bench by Frasquita, wife of
the miller Lucas, because he annoys her with his attentions. Lucas, hidden in the arbor by his wife, laughs at the
discomfort of Zeniga who vows vengeance. Lucas is bid-
den to appear before the magistrate. Zeniga, dripping wet
from a fall into the pond, comes to the mill and tries to
make love to Frasquita, who threatens him with her husband's musket. Zeniga puts on the clothes of the miller,
who just then returns, his summons being a hoax to get
him out of the way, and finds Zeniga in his wife's bed-
room, although alone. Lucas, to get even, goes to Zeniga's
house and tries to make love to Donna Zeniga. He is sound-
ly thrashed. Zeniga, in the meantime, decides to stay at
home and make love to his own wife, so that all is well,
and Lucas and Frasquita return happily to the mill.

La Fiamma	Respighi
(The Flame)	(1879-1936)

Première: Rome, 1934.
Première: Chicago, 1935, with Rosa Raisa as Silvana,
  Sonia Sharnova as Agnes (the Witch), Carlo
  Morelli as Basilio, Bentonelli as Donello, Marie
  Barova as Eudossia. The composer conducted.
  Berlin, 1936.

59

Italian

Tragic opera in three acts and final scene.
Story based on *The Witch*, a drama by H. W. Jensen.
Libretto by Gyastalla.
Action: Ravenna, seventh century.

Silvana, the young second wife of Basilio, and her mother-in-law, Eudossia, are in disagreement, when an old hag, Agnes di Cervia, rushes in and asks protection from a mob which accuses her of the death of a man through sorcery. Silvana conceals her. Donello, the young son of Basilio arrives for a visit and he and Silvana recognize each other although they have not met since childhood. The mob enters, finds Agnes and as she is dragged out she intimates that some day Silvana will have the same experience. In her death agony she discloses that Silvana's mother had the same power of sorcery. Basilio hearing of this confesses to Silvana that her mother had bewitched him into marrying her. Silvana tries the strange power she feels and brings Donello to her. When her mother-in-law discovers their guilty love, Silvana confesses to her husband her love for his son. The husband drops dead. She is accused of sorcery. When she tries to take the oath of innocence she is unable to speak, and is burned at the stake.

Il Dybbuk	Lodovico Rocca
(A Demon Soul)	(1898-)

Première: Milan, Turin, Warsaw, 1934.
Première: Rome, 1935.
Première: Detroit, Michigan, 1936.
Première: New York, Carnegie Hall, 1936, with Rosa
 Raisa as Leah, Frederick Jagel as Hanan.

Lyric drama with prologue and three acts. Libretto by Simoni.

Story founded on the Hebrew drama, *Rappaport of Vitebsk*, by Sholom Anski. English translation by Archie Coates.

Leah, daughter of Sender, and Hanan, son of Nissen, are at birth pledged in marriage by their parents. But Sender becomes rich and desires a rich husband for his daughter, while Nissen dies poor and his son, Hanan, becomes a deep student of the Talmud, searching for wisdom in the temple. Leah and Hanan meet and love. While they are together Sender gaily enters and announces that he has found the proper husband for his daughter. Hanan falls dead, book in hand. On the day of the wedding, just as the bridal wreath is being placed on Leah's head, she shrieks and a voice comes from within her. The Dybbuk, which has entered her body, cries out that she has been promised to him—he has come to claim her and will never leave her. Sender is horrified and begs the Rabbi to dispossess his daughter of the evil spirit. Hanan's shadow appears. He takes Leah's soul from her body. As she expires voices are heard crying that what was recorded has come to pass.

NOTE: According to Hebrew lore, a dybbuk is a disembodied spirit that takes possession of a living body.

La Favola del Figlio Cambiato	Malipiero
(Legend of the Changeling Son)	(1882-)

Première: Brunswick, Germany, 1934.

61

Italian

Legendary music drama in three acts and five scenes. Text by Pirandello.

This is the old story of the changing of the King's son and the son of a beggar and has to do with the soul turmoil and instinct of a betrayed mother. The real Prince is deformed and degenerate, living among the human scum of bar-rooms and river docks. The false Prince lives among the beautiful and gentle things of life but longs for the happiness that comes from being of service to others. The enigma is finally solved and all ends happily.

Liola   Guiseppe Mule
                                                        (1885-   )

Première: Naples, 1935.
Première: Turin, 1936. Conducted by the composer.
Lyric comedy opera in three acts. Libretto by Rossato
     after Pirandello's play. A lively and realistic picture of rural life on the island of Sicily.

Liola is a handsome and attractive peasant who is a veritable Don Juan. He has been the ruin of many trusting girls. However, the last is the buxom Tuzza, who refuses his proposal of marriage, though about to bear his child. An old man, Simon, longs for an heir he can never have and has thrown out his young wife because she has no child. The old man is rich and Liola hits upon a plan to get some of the old man's wealth. He makes the old man think he is the father of Tuzza's coming child. The old

62

man takes back his wife, reconciles Liola and Tuzza, pays their marriage expenses and all live happily together ever after.

NOTE: Pirandello has disowned this operatic Liola because of the many changes made by the librettist.

Nerone   Mascagni
                                         (1863-   )

Première: Milan, 1935. The composer conducted.
     Libretto by Tozzetti.
Tragic opera in three acts and four scenes. No prelude.
The plot is after a play by Pietro Cossa.
Action: Rome in the time of Nero, about 66 A. D.

A very beautiful intermezzo occurs between the two
     scenes in the last act.

A motley crowd of men, merchants, slaves, gladiators, etc., is gathered in a tavern drinking and cursing Nero for his cruel barbarism. Egloge, a beautiful Greek slave runs in and begs protection from two men who have molested her. The crowd gives the men a sound beating and is in terror when one of them proves to be Nero himself. He puts out the crowd and sends Egloge to his palace. Atte, a freed woman who loves him, warns him that Rome is about to fall. Nero falls in love with Egloge and makes her his queen. During an orgy in the palace Egloge is poisoned by a rival and dies. Nero hears that the people are revolting. He escapes and hides in a hut belonging to one of his followers, but when he learns that he is pronounced an enemy he falls on his sword and dies.

63

XXth CENTURY OPERA

Italian

Orseolo   Pizzetti
(1880-   )

Première: Florence, 1935.
Première: Turin, 1936.
Legendary romantic opera in three acts. Text by composer. The story depicts the conflict between aristocracy and democracy.
Action: Venice, seventeenth century.

Marco Orseolo, a patrician, is being conspired against by the new-rich clan of Renieri Fusiner, which kidnaps Orseolo's daughter, Contarina and falls in love with her. She returns his love and their marriage unites the interests of both classes, high and low.

La Fiera   Mario Cremesini

Première: Florence, 1935.
Lyric comedy in two acts. Libretto by Bonelli. Based on the witty play, *La Fiera dell Impruneta*, by Bucciolini. This is a gay love intrigue offering sentimental and comic themes.
Action: Impruneta, a typical Tuscan hill village near Florence, during the annual cattle fair of St. Lukes, seventeenth century.

Leonardo   Riccardo Storti
(1875-   )

Première: Rome, 1935.
Romantic opera in three acts. Libretto by Antonio Lega.

Action: Italy and France, about 1500.

Deals with episodes in the life of the great painter Leonardo da Vinci, centering around the beautiful Mona Lisa (La Giaconda), the wife of Francesco del Giocondo—the subject of da Vinci's famous painting in the Louvre.

Julius Caesar   Malipiero
                                           (1882-   )
Première: Genoa, 1936.
Tragic music drama in three acts and seven scenes.
Text by the composer, after Shakespeare's tragedy.
Action: Rome. The battlefield of Phillipi.

Act I *Scene 1* — A street in Rome. A soothsayer accosts Caesar and warns him of the Ides of March.
       Scene 2 — Brutus' orchard. The conspirators plan the death of Caesar.
Act II *Scene 1* — Caesar's palace. Caesar's wife begs him not to go to the Senate. She has a premonition of evil.
       Scene 2 — The Senate. Caesar is assassinated.
Act III *Scene 1* — Caesar's funeral.
       Scene 2 — Rioting of the people.
       Scene 3 — The Battlefield. Brutus and Cassius are killed in battle on the plain of Phillipi.

Cyrano de Bergerac   Franco Alfano
                                           (1876-   )
Première: Rome, 1936.
Première: Paris, 1936.

65

Romantic opera in four acts and five scenes.
After the play by Edmond Rostand. Italian version by Caesare Meano and Fillippo Brusa. A sword and cloak romance.
Action: Paris and environs, 1640 A.D.

Cyrano of the huge nose is hopelessly in love with his cousin Roxane. One of her suitors, De Guiche, insults him about his nose and they fight a duel. Cyrano learns that Roxane is in love with his friend Christian. He gives up his love and writes to her sonnets and love letters for Christian who is slow of speech. He finally gets the lovers safely married. When Cyrano is mortally wounded the truth comes out. Roxane has been wooed and won by Cyrano *for Christian*.

Il Campiello   Wolf-Ferrari
                                                      (1876-   )
Première: Milan, 1936.
Première: Rome, 1937.
Première: Dresden, 1937.
Lyric comic opera in three acts. Libretto by Mario Ghisalberti. Based on a comedy by Goldoni.
Action: Venice, eighteenth century.

"Il Campiello is an extraordinary portrayal of the typical life of a small Venetian square, in all the intimate realism of its gossips and quarrels, its loves and jealousies, its plea-

66

sures and foibles benevolently observed. The plot interest is submerged in a miracle of local color."

(Raymond Hall in the *New York Times*, Feb. 21, 1936)

The music is charming and amusing from beginning to end.

Miranda   Pietro Canonica
                                                    (1869-   )

Première: San Remo, Italy, 1937.
Lyric drama in three acts.
Libretto by Carlo Bernardi after Shakespeare's
    Tempest.

Prospero, the rightful Duke of Milan, dethroned by his brother Antonio, is put to sea in a leaky boat with his little daughter, the three-year-old Miranda. They land on a fairy island, on which lives the hideous Caliban. Prospero, using his knowledge of magic, wields his power over Caliban and Ariel, leader of all the spirits on the island, and keeps them under his spell. Years afterward, Antonio and many of his friends come to the island on a ship. Prospero uses his magic and a violent storm wrecks the vessel. All are spellbound to find Prospero and Miranda and in time Ferdinand, son of the King of Naples, and Miranda fall in love. Prospero is restored to his title and all ends well.

NOTE: Pietro Canonica is a sculptor of Turin and is noted for his busts of many crowned heads.

67

Italian

Lucretia   Respighi
(1879-1936)

Première: Milan, 1937.
Tragic opera in one act. Libretto by Claudia Gustalla,
    after Livy's story.
Action: Ancient Rome, about 500 B.C.

Posthumous opera of the composer. Finished by his wife,
    Elsa, who was his pupil and is herself a composer.

According to Roman legend, Lucretia, the virtuous wife
of King Tarquinius (the Proud), was dishonored by Sex-
tus, the youngest son of Tarquinius Superbus. She im-
plored her father and her husband to avenge her disgrace
and then stabbed herself. This caused a revolution which
resulted in the expulsion of the tyrannical Tarquinius from
Rome and the establishment of a republic in place of the
kingdom.

Paul and Virginia   Giandrea Gavazzeni
(1909-   )

Première: Bergamo, Italy, 1935.
Lyric tragedy in one act of three scenes. Libretto by
    Mario Ghisalberti.
After the classic of Bernadin de St. Pierre.
Action: Port Louis. In the Mauritius.

Paul, the illegitimate son of Margaret (who has hidden
herself on the island to get away from the world), and
Virginia, daughter of a French widow, were playmates
from childhood and were brought up without knowledge

68

of the outside world. Their childhood affection develops into love, when Virginia's aunt adopts her and takes her to France. After two years, when she refuses to marry the person of her aunt's choice, she is sent back to her mother. Within a short distance of the island the ship is wrecked and Virginia is drowned. Paul sees the tragedy from the shore and slowly dies of grief.

Amelia al Ballo	Gian-Carlo Menotti
(Amelia Goes to the Ball)	(1912-)

Première: Philadelphia, Curtis Institute of Music, at Academy of Music, 1937, with Margaret Daum as Amelia, Conrad Mayo as the Husband, William Martin as the Lover, Leonard Treash as the Chief of Police.

Première: New York, Metropolitan Opera House, 1938, with Muriel Dickson as Amelia, John Brownlee as the Husband, Mario Chamlee as the Lover, Norman Cordon as the Chief of Police.

Opera bouffe in one act.

Libretto by the composer, who characterizes it as a whimsical satire on women. English translation by George Mead.

Action: Milan, 1900.

Amelia is making preparations for attending a grand ball when her husband enters with a letter which he has intercepted from Amelia's lover. He promises to take her to the ball if she will tell him her lover's name. When he

Italian

learns that the lover lives on the next floor, he rushes out to shoot him. Amelia, from her balcony, warns the lover and conceals him when they hear the husband returning. The lover is discovered, but since he is a strong young man, the husband consents to talk over the situation. Amelia, tired of waiting to go to the ball, breaks a vase over her husband's head. This knocks him unconscious and Amelia begins to scream, accusing her lover of being a burglar and that he had attacked her husband. The lover is arrested, the husband sent to the hospital, and Amelia goes to the ball—with the Chief of Police ! !

ITALIAN OPERA

(PART II)

composed *before 1900*

and presented for the *first time*

in the United States, during the

*XX*TH *Century*

(in prominent opera houses)

also

Outstanding revivals in the

United States during the same period.

1900 — Season 1937–1938

(inclusive)

Italian

La Boheme   Puccini
                                             (1858-1924)
Première: Turin, Italy, 1896.
Première: Buenos Aires, 1896.
Première: San Francisco, Calif., 1898.
Première: New York, Metropolitan Opera House,
      1900, with Melba as Mimi, Albert Saleza as Ru-
      dolph, Campanari as Marcel, Gillibert as Schunard,
      Journet as Colline.
Tragic opera in four acts.
Plot founded on H. Murger's book, *Bohemian Life.*
Libretto by Illica and Giacosa.
Action: Paris, 1830.

   This is a story of Bohemian student life in Paris. Four
friends, Marcel, Rudolph, Colline and Schunard live in an
attic studio. Marcel paints; Rudolph kindles the fire with
MSS which Colline could not sell. There is a knock at the
door and Mimi is revealed and faints on the threshold. She
lives in the house and has lost her key which Rudolph
finds and hides so as to keep her. They live quite happily
for a time and then Mimi goes away. One day she comes
back to die. They arrange a bed for her. She begs Rudolph
not to leave her and she dies in his arms.

NOTE: After six years' absence Bori returned to the Metropolitan
as Mimi in 1921.

   La Fille du Regiment   Donizetti
   (Daughter of the Regiment)   (1797-1848)
Première: Paris, 1840.

Première: New Orleans, 1843.
Première: New York, Metropolitan Opera House,
    1902, with Sembrich as Marie, Salignac as Tonio,
    Gillibert as the Sergeant.
Military comic opera in two acts.
Libretto by Gollmick.
From the French of Bayard and St. Georges.
Action: Swiss Tyrol, 1815.

Marie, a baby found on the battlefield by Sergeant Sul-
pizio, is adopted by his regiment. She loves a farmer boy,
Tonio, who saved her from falling over a precipice, and
they are to be married. However, she proves to be the long
lost niece of a Countess, who takes her to her castle. Marie
pines for Tonio but her Aunt wishes her to marry a titled
man. But Tonio, now an army officer, comes to claim her
for his bride. The Countess consents and all ends happily.

Iris   Mascagni
                                 (1863-   )
Première: Rome, 1898.
Première: New York Metropolitan Opera House,
    1902, when the composer conducted his own opera
    company with Marie Farneti as Iris.
Première: Revival 1908 with the Metropolitan Opera
    Company; Eames as Iris, Caruso as Osaka, Scotti
    as Kyoto, Journet as Cieco (the blind father).
Oriental tragic opera in three acts.
Libretto by Luiga Illica.
Action: Japan, nineteenth century.

Iris, playing with her doll, is fancied by the rich young Osaka, who has her abducted. She wakes up in a house of ill fame and Osaka is disgusted with her innocence. He orders Kyoto to sell her as a slave. Her blind father curses her and she throws herself into the sewer and drowns as she listens to the voice of the divine Sun and is welcomed into the Japanese Paradise.

L' Elisir d' Amore   Donizetti
(Elixir of Love)   (1797-1848)

Première: Milan, 1832.
Première: New York, 1838. Park Theatre.
Première: New Orleans, La., 1842.
Première: New York, Metropolitan Opera House,
       1903, with Sembrich as Adina, Caruso as Nemo-
       rino, Scotti as Belcore (the soldier), Rossi as the
       quack Doctor.
Comic opera in two acts. Text by Romani.
Action: Small Italian village, early nineteenth century.

Adina and her farmer-boy lover Nemorino are quite happy until a dashing young soldier appears on the scene. Poor Nemorino drinks a love potion thinking to bring Adina back to him. Instead of a love potion it is wine and makes him drunk. Adina is quite disgusted and so decides to marry the soldier. Nemorino enlists as a soldier and Adina finds that she loves him after all and buys his freedom. So they wed and all ends happily.

AT HOME AND ABROAD
Italian

Fedora   Giordano
                                              (1867-   )

Première: Milan, 1898.
Première: New York, Metropolitan Opera House,
    1906, with Cavalieri as Fedora, Caruso as Count
    Ispanov.
Tragic opera in three acts.
Story after Sardou's play tells of Russian police horrors
    under the Czar.
Action: Petrograd and environs, Paris, nineteenth
    century.

   Fedora, betrothed to Count Vladimir, is waiting for
him in his drawing-room when he is brought in mortally
wounded. A certain Count Ispanov is the assassin. Fedora
plans revenge. She meets and fascinates Ispanov in Paris
and tells him she is returning to Russia. He declares he
cannot follow her as he had committed a crime in Russia
and cannot return. He had killed Vladimir because he
(Vladimir) had seduced his wife. He and Fedora repair
to her villa. Her spy has caused the death of Ispanov's
brother and the shock has killed his aged mother. Fedora
in bitter remorse drinks poison and falls into the arms of
the unhappy Ispanov.

NOTE: Edward Johnson made his operatic debut as Count Ispanov
in Chicago in 1919.

Andrea Chenier   Giordano
                                              (1867-   )

Première: Milan, 1896.

75

Italian

Première: New York, Academy of Music, 1896.

Première: New York, Manhattan Opera House, 1908, with Eva Tetrazzini as Madeleine, Sammarco as Gerard, Bassi as Andrea.

Première: Metropolitan Opera House for the first time, 1920, with Claudia Muzio as Madeleine, Beniamino Gigli as Andrea, Giuseppe Danise as Gerard.

Tragic opera in four acts. Libretto by Illica, using the historical character, Andrea Chenier, as a basis for the plot.

Action: Paris, before and during the Revolution.

Andrea Chenier, the poet, loves Madeleine and she returns his love. They are in sympathy with the starving people. Gerard, a leader of the Revolution, also loves Madeleine. Gerard and Andrea cross swords. Gerard is wounded. Andrea is imprisoned and is to be executed. Madeleine pleads in vain for his life. She bribes the jailer to let her take the place of a woman on the death list and she and Andrea die together.

NOTE: Mme. Eva Tetrazzini, who had retired from the stage, sang this performance as a tribute to her husband, Cleofonte Campanini, the brilliant conductor of the Manhattan Opera Company, in whose honor this gala performance was given (Manhattan Opera House, 1908.)

Manon Lescaut   Puccini
                                                (1858-1924)
Première: Turin, 1893.

Première: New York, 1898, by an Italian Opera Company.

AT HOME AND ABROAD
Italian

Première: New York, Metropolitan Opera House,
    1907, with Cavalieri as Manon, Caruso as des
    Grieux.
Tragic opera in four acts.
Plot after Abbe Prevost's novel.
Action: Paris and vicinity; Louisiana; 1721.

Manon knows no law but the dictates of her own heart.
She leaves her lover Grieux and becomes the mistress of
the rich Geronte. Des Grieux begs her to return to him,
which she does and takes with her the jewels she feels she
has earned. Geronte has her arrested for theft and she is
imprisoned awaiting deportation to America. Des Grieux
is allowed to board the ship and goes with her to Louisiana.
Here on an open plain she dies in his arms.

NOTE: Puccini was present at a Philadelphia production in English
in 1894.

Lucretia Bori made her American debut in the title role at the
Metropolitan in 1912, with Caruso singing des Grieux.

NOTE: Mme. Frances Alda made her farewell Metropolitan appearance in December 1929 as Manon with Gigli as des Grieux.

Crispino e la Comare   Luigi Ricci (1805-1859)
(The Cobbler and the Fairy)   F. Ricci (1809-1877)

Première: Venice, 1850.
Première: New York, 1884. Academy of Music.

77

Italian

Première: New York, 1908, Manhattan Opera House, with Luisa Tetrazzini as Annetta, Gianoli Galletti as Crispino, Emma Zaccaria as the Fairy, Mario Sammarco as Dr. Fabrizio.

Première: New York Metropolitan Opera House, 1919, with Frieda Hempel as Annetta, Scotti as Crispino, Sophie Braslau as the Fairy, Thos. Chalmers as Dr. Fabrizio.

Opera bouffe in three acts. Book by Francesco Marie Piave.

Story after fairy tale by Carlo Gozzie.

Action: Venice, seventeenth century.

Crispino, his wife, Annetta, and their children are starving. A fairy appears and tells him to hang out a doctor's shingle. He does so and cures a rich man whom all the doctors had given up. Crispino becomes rich and proud and unkind to his wife and children. In a dream he sees the good fairy's face turn to a skeleton head as she points him to a candle about to go out (himself), and another (Annetta) burning brightly. He wakes a changed man—kind, humble and-grateful for his good wife and children.

La Forza del Destino	Verdi
(Force of Destiny)	(1813-1901)

Première: St. Petersburg, 1862.
Première: New York, 1865, Academy of Music.

Première: New York, Metropolitan Opera House,
  1918, with Rosa Ponselle (her debut in opera) as
  Leonora, Caruso as Don Alvaro, de Luca as Don
  Carlos.
Tragic opera in four acts.
Story after De Riva's drama, *Don Alvaro o la Fuera del
  Sino.*
Action: Spain and Italy, eighteenth century.

Don Alvaro, in love with Leonora, daughter of Marquis
Calatrava, accidentally kills her father. Leonora seeks the
advice of the kindly abbot and is directed to a cave where
she may live unmolested and under the protection of the
monks of the monastery. Her brother, Don Carlos, enters
the army under an assumed name. So does Don Alvaro.
They become fast friends. Don Carlos, discovering the
identity of Don Alvaro, challenges him to a duel and is
wounded, apparently fatally. Don Alvaro enters the monastery under the name of Father Raphael. Don Carlos recovers and seeks out Alvaro and challenges him. They
fight near the retreat of Leonora, who rushes out, recognizes Don Alvaro and her brother. She leans over Don
Carlos, who is dying. He stabs her. She dies. Don Alvaro
leaps over the precipice to his death.

Cosi fan tutte	Mozart
(School for lovers)	(1756-1791)

Première: Vienna, 1790.
Première: New York Metropolitan Opera House,
  1922, with Florence Easton as Fiordiligi, Frances

Italian

Peratta as Dorabella, Lucrezia Bori as Despina, George Meader as "Ferrando," de Luca as Guglielmo, Didur as Alfonso.

Comic opera in two acts and seven tableaux. Text by Ponte. Depicts feminine faithfulness in spite of intrigues.

Action: Naples, eighteenth century.

The pessimistic bachelor Alfonso hears his friends, Ferrando and Guglielmo, praising the beauty of their sweethearts, Dorabella and Fiordiligi. They make a wager with Alfonso that he cannot make them unfaithful. Alfonso disguises the lovers and introduces them to the maids under false names. The maids are a little coy with the new beaux but the joke is soon revealed and they admit they have been foolish, so all ends well.

NOTE: Metropolitan Opera House, 1922, the U. S. Première of the opera.

Luisa Miller   Verdi
                                              (1813-1901)

Première: Naples, 1849.
Première: Philadelphia, 1852.
Première: New York, Academy of Music, 1886.
Première: New York Metropolitan Opera House,
          1929, with Rosa Ponselle as Luisa, Lauri-Volpi as
          Rodolfo, de Luca as Count Walter, Marion Telva
          as the Duchess.

Tragic opera in three acts. Libretto by Cammarano.

AT HOME AND ABROAD
Italian

Story after Schiller's play, *Kabale und Liebe*.
Action: A Tyrolean village, early seventeenth century.

Rodolfo loves Luisa, but his father, Count Walter, insists on his marrying the Duchess of Ostheim. To rescue her father, who is imprisoned by the Count's demand, Luisa sends him a letter saying she releases Rodolfo and will marry another. Rodolfo, shocked by this decision, agrees to marry the Duchess but goes to Luisa's home. He poisons a cup from which they both drink, when she tells him the truth, and they die together.

Il Signor Bruschino   Rossini
                                             (1792-1868)

Première: Venice, 1813.
Première: New York, Metropolitan Opera House,
     1932, with Fleischer as Sofia, Tokyatan as Floville,
     Pinza as Gaudenzio, de Luca as Bruschino (the
     elder).
Comic opera in one act. Book by Guiseppe Foppa.
Action: Somewhere in Italy, early nineteenth century.

Floville loves Sofia, whose guardian, Gaudenzio is the enemy of Floville's father. Gaudenzio would have Sofia marry the son of the gouty old aristocrat Bruschino. But the young son is a scamp who never pays his bills and is just now held prisoner by an inn-keeper until he pays what he owes him. Floville decides to impersonate the son, and before Gaudenzio discovers the plot, he has united

81

the two lovers. The old aristocrat is left to settle up with the wayward son as best he may.

NOTE: The Metropolitan production of 1932 was the American première of the Opera.

Simon Boccanegra   Verdi
                                              (1813-1901)

Première: Venice, 1857, when it was a failure. Milan
    revival, 1887, a great success.
Première: New York, Metropolitan Opera House,
    1932, with Tibbett as Simon, Maria Müller as
    Amelia, Martinelli as Gabriele, Pinza as Fiesco,
    Claudio Frigerio as Paolo. This was the American
    première of the opera.
Tragic opera with prologue and three acts.
Book by Piave, after a Spanish drama.
Action: Italy, fourteenth century.

Simon Boccanegra, a brave young peasant who has cleared the sea of pirates, is, as a reward, made Doge of Venice. He hesitates to be in the patrician class, but as Doge he can marry Maria, daughter of Fiesco, leader of the patricians. Simon loves her and she has borne him a daughter, but is imprisoned by her father in his castle. Just as Simon is made Doge, Maria dies, her child is stolen and the old nurse murdered. Twenty-five years pass. Amelia Grimaldi is betrothed to Gabriele, a Genoese nobleman. Simon recognizes in her his long-lost daughter

82

and refuses the request of Paolo for her hand. Paolo in anger swears revenge. He arouses Gabriele's jealousy by suggesting that Simon loves Amelia. Gabriele witnesses a tender scene between the father and daughter, and leaps into the room, dagger in hand. When he learns their true relationship he becomes an ardent defender of Simon. While preparations are being made for the marriage of Amelia and Gabriele, Paolo poisons the Doge. Simon dies, giving his blessing to his daughter and her lover.

Secret Marriage	Domenico Cimarosa
(Matrimonio Segreto)	(1749-1801)

Première: Vienna, 1792.
Première: New York, 1834, Italian Opera House.
Première: New York, 1933, Juilliard Opera School.
Première: First time at Metropolitan Opera House,
      1937, with Muriel Dickson as Caroline, Natalie
      Bodanya as Elsietta, George Rasely as Paolino,
      Huhn as Count Robinson.
Comic opera in two acts and three scenes. Libretto by
      Bertati. English translation by Reginald Gatty and
      Albert Stoessel.
Action: Naples, eighteenth century.

    Paolino, a poor lawyer, is secretly married to Caroline, a rich man's daughter. He introduces a rich friend, Count Robinson, to Caroline's sister Elsietta, hoping to make a match. The Count falls in love with Caroline to the delight of her father, but the consternation of the married pair. Paolino and Caroline decide to elope but are

83

caught. The Count finds that it is Elsietta after all that he loves and all ends well.

NOTE: This is considered the third best comic opera ever written, —*Marriage of Figaro* being first, *Barber of Seville*, second.

Linda de Chamounix   Donizetti
                                                       (1798-1848)
Première: Vienna, 1842.
Première: New York, 1847. Astor Place.
Première: New York, 1883, Academy of Music.
    Adelina Patti sang a special performance as Linda at the Metropolitan Opera House in 1890, but the opera was not included in the repertoire of the Metropolitan until 1934, when Lily Pons sang Linda, Richard Crooks, Carlo (Arthur), de Luca, Antonio (Linda's father).
Romantic opera in three acts. Book by Proch.
Action: Chamounix and Paris, about 1760.

Linda is pursued by a wicked marquis, and her father sends her to Paris to escape him. She is in love with Carlo, a young artist who has been painting the mountains near her home. Carlo follows her to Paris and reveals himself as a wealthy noble. He persuades her to occupy the apartment he provides for her, while he gains the consent of his family to marry her. The father, Antonio, comes to Paris and seeing the luxury in which she is living, wrongly accuses her and leaves. She becomes insane, wanders back to Chamounix and there her lover finds her. His family has consented to their marriage. Linda's reason is restored and all ends happily.

84

La Serva Padrona	Pergolesi
(Maid or Mistress)	(1710-1736)

Première: Naples, 1731.
Première: New York, Metropolitan Opera House,
   1935, (American Première), with Edith Fleischer
   as Serpina, Louis D'Angelo as Pandolfo.
Comic opera in two acts. Text by Nelli.
Action: Naples, eighteenth century.

In every way she knows, Serpina, maid to Pandolfo, has tried to make her master think he wants to marry her, but he is quite satisfied to have her see to his comfort in the capacity of maid. She finally resorts to a clever trick to make him jealous. The trick succeeds and he proposes to her. So that she becomes mistress of his house after all.

NOTE: Held as a model for Italian *Opera Buffa* for generations.

Il Maestro di Musica	Pergolesi
(Music Master)	(1710-1736)

Première: Naples, 1731.
Première: Philadelphia, 1937, (American Première),
   with Marie Zara as Lauretta, Fritz Kreuger as
   Lamberto, Edward Rheim as Colagianni.
Chamber comedy in two acts.

The story deals with the amorous and professional rivalry of Lamberto, a singing teacher, and Colagianni, an

85

Italian

impresario, over the would-be prima donna, Lauretta, who cleverly handles both men for her own professional advancement.

NOTE: Mephisto in the issue of Musical America for March 25, 1937, remarks that Boston claims the American Première in 1936.

Othello   Verdi
                                        (1813-1901)

Première: Milan, 1887.
Première: New York, 1888. Academy of Music.
    Notable performance at Metropolitan Opera House, 1902, with Eames as Desdemona, Alvarez as Othello, Scotti as Iago, Louise Homer as Emilia.
Tragic opera in four acts. Text by Boito, after Shakespeare.
Action: Seaport in Cyprus. End of fifteenth century.

Iago hates Othello, but he pretends loyalty. He devises a plot to incite jealousy in the heart of Othello toward his devoted wife, Desdemona. Iago causes Othello to deprive Cassio of his lieutenancy. Cassio approaches the gentle Desdemona, begging her intercession with Othello, to be reinstated. Iago draws Othello to the window to see them talking together in the garden and warns him to watch his wife. Othello becomes madly jealous. Iago succeeds in making him believe Desdemona false. He finally smothers her to death, while she protests her innocence. Emilia has discovered the wickedness of her husband, Iago, and de-

86

clares the innocence of Desdemona. Iago flees. Othello,
full of remorse, stabs himself and dies.

NOTE: There was a brilliant revival at the Paris Opera and at
Covent Garden in 1937, with Lawrence Tibbett as Iago, Martinelli
as Othello, and Eide Norena as Desdemona. It was sung at the
Metropolitan on December 22nd of that year, after an absence of
24 seasons, with the same male cast, Mme. Rethberg singing Desdemona, at a last-minute notice owing to the illness of Mme.
Norena.

Rigoletto   Verdi
                                                   (1813-1901)
Première: Venice, 1851.
Première: New York, 1855. Academy of Music.
Première: New York, 1870. Stadt Theatre.
Première: New York, Metropolitan Opera House,
        1883.
        Notable revival, Metropolitan Opera House, 1903,
        at which Caruso made his Metropolitan debut as
        the Duke, Sembrich sang Gilda, Homer, Madda-
        lena, Scotti, Rigoletto.
Tragic opera in three acts. Text by Piave after Hugo's
        drama, *Le Roi S' Amuse.*
Action: Mantua and vicinity, sixteenth century.

The licentious Duke of Mantua deceives and betrays
Gilda, the lovely daughter of Rigoletto, the King's fool.
Gilda still believes in his love though it is proven that he
is false to her. Her father plots to have the Duke killed
and his body delivered to him in a bag. Gilda outside the

87

Italian

inn hears the Duke singing a mocking song. She goes into the inn and is killed instead of the Duke. When Rigoletto opens the bag which is delivered to him, he finds the body of his beloved daughter, Gilda, who has gladly given her life for her lover.

NOTE: Frances Alda made her Metropolitan debut as Gilda in 1908.

La Sonnambula   Bellini
(Sleep-walker)   (1801-1835)

Première: Milan, 1831.
Première: New York, Park Theatre, 1835.
Première: New York, Palmo's Opera House, 1844.
    Noteworthy revival Metropolitan Opera House, 1905, with Sembrich as Amina, Caruso as Elvino. Plancon as Rodolfo.
Lyric opera in two acts. Book by Felice Romani.
Action: A Swiss village.

Walking in her sleep, Amina roams the village at night. She goes into the inn and lies in the bed of a young lord, Rodolfo, who, finding her there leaves immediately. The innkeeper however, calls in the whole village to see the girl asleep in a strange man's bed. Her village lover, Elvino, tears his ring from her finger, when she wakes. The village folk and her lover are finally convinced that she is a sleep-walker and all ends happily.

88

AT HOME AND ABROAD

Italian

Aida	Verdi
	(1813-1901)

Première: Cairo, Egypt, 1871. (Composed for the
    Khedive of Egypt for the opening of his Grand
    Opera House, in celebration of the dedication of
    the Suez Canal.
Première: New York, 1873, Academy of Music.
    Famous revival, Metropolitan Opera House, 1908,
    the initiatory opera of Gatti-Cazzaza's regime,
    with Emmy Destinn in her United States debut, as
    Aida, Homer as Amneris, Caruso as Rhadames,
    Scotti as Amonasro. This was also the United
    States debut of Toscanini as conductor.
Tragic opera in four acts. Book by Ghislanzoni and the
    composer from the French of du Locle.
Story by Mariette Bey, the Egyptologist.
Action: Memphis and Thebes in the time of the
    Pharaohs.

    Aida, daughter of an Ethiopian King, Amonasro, is a
slave in Pharaoh's palace. Amneris, daughter of Pharaoh,
is in love with Rhadames, who in turn loves Aida and is
loved by her. Amonasro is brought as captive to the King
and is held as hostage, while the other prisoners are set
free at Rhadames' request. Amonasro persuades Aida to
extract from her lover information which will be of use
to the Ethiopians, unfolding a plan by which she and
Rhadames may flee together. Amneris overhears when

89

Aida reveals the plan to Rhadames and the information which Aida has tricked him into giving. Rhadames is condemned to be buried alive. Aida secretes herself in the tomb and they die together.

Orfeo ed Eurydice   Gluck
(1714-1787)

Première: Vienna, 1762. Conducted by composer.
Première: New York, Winter Garden, 1863.
Première: New York, 1909, Metropolitan Opera
     House, noted revival, with Louise Homer as
     Orpheus, Johanna Gadski as Eurydice, Alma
     Gluck as the Happy Spirit, Bella Alten as Amor.
     Toscanini conducted.
Classic Music Drama in four acts. Book by Calzabigi,
     from the Greek legend.

Eurydice, lovely wife of Orpheus, is killed by the sting of a serpent. The sorrowing Orpheus gains the pity of the Gods through the magic of his music drawn from his lyre. He is allowed to bring his wife back from the underworld upon one condition—that he shall not gaze into her face until they are back on the earth. He succeeds in finding Eurydice and brings her from the Elysian Fields, but she pleads so hard that he should look at her that he forgets his promise and, alas, she is again lost to him. But the god of love in pity restores her to him and they burst into songs of praise to the gods as they reach the earth.

FRENCH OPERA

(PART I)

composed and produced abroad,

in the United States, or in both,

during the

XXTH *Century*

1900 — Season 1937–1938

(inclusive)

Character of French Opera

With the entrance of Italian opera into France, its ideas
were speedily grafted on the French ballet. Scenic effects, vocal and dramatic demands, fixed the standard
of French grand opera. Here again the touch of
Gluck's opera reform is seen. Building upon the former
work of Lully and Rameau, he raised the standard of
opera in France and established the form of French
grand opera.

91

French

Louise   Gustave Charpentier
                                                  (1860-   )

Première: Paris, 1900.

Première: New York, 1907, Manhattan Opera House, with Mary Garden as Louise, Charles Dalmores as Julien, Mme. Bressler-Gianoli as the Mother, Charles Gillibert as the Father.

Première: New York, 1921, Metropolitan Opera House, with Farrar as Louise, Orville Harrold as Julien, Mme. Berat as the Mother, Clarence White-hill as the Father.

Romantic opera in four acts.

Story by the composer, depicts Bohemian life in Paris.

Action: Paris, present time.

Louise, an honest sewing-girl, lives with her parents in humble quarters in the Paris tenement section. Julien, a young poet, lives in a garret across the street, which is quite narrow. Louise's mother finds them flirting from their windows and warns her daughter to have nothing to do with him. Julien meets Louise on the way to her work and begs her to go away with him, but she refuses. He serenades her in the sewing-shop. She leaves her work and goes off with him. At home she quarrels with her father when he tells her that Julien is dissolute. She leaves home and joins Julien. When her father is dying her mother begs her to come home. She sits beside her father's bed and they beg her not to return to Julien, but she says she must be free to do as she likes and cries out wildly for Julien. Her father curses her and pushes her out of the room. She rushes into the street and back to Julien, never to return to her parents.

92

Griselidis   Massenet
       (1842-1912)

Première: Paris, 1901.

Première: New York, 1910, Manhattan Opera House, with Mary Garden as Griselidis, Hector Dufranne as her Crusader husband, Marquis de Saluces, Gustave Huberdeau as the Devil.

Miracle music drama with prologue and three acts.

Based on modern mystery play by Sylvestre and Moraud.

Action: Provence, France, thirteenth century.

Griselidis is the wife of a Crusader, a hero who trusts and loves her. As he leaves for the Crusades he unwisely wagers the devil that nothing can tempt his wife to be unfaithful. The devil brings a former admirer to her garden, a handsome young shepherd who attempts to make love to her but is interrupted by her little son. Angered by his interruption the devil steals the boy, promising to return him if Griselidis will kiss him (the devil). She refuses. When the husband returns the devil tries to prove her unfaithfulness but without success. Husband and wife go to the chapel to pray for the return of their son. A great light fills the altar and the boy is seen standing before the figure of a saint. The devil is overcome and the parents clasp their child in their arms in gratitude.

Le Jongleur de Notre Dame   Massenet
  (Juggler of Notre Dame)   (1842-1912)

Première: Monte Carlo, 1902.

93

French

Première: New York, Manhattan Opera House, 1908,
with Mary Garden as Jean, Maurice Renaud as
Boniface the cook, Hector Dufranne as the Prior.
Miracle opera in three acts.
Libretto by Maurice Lena, after a medieval play by
Anatole France.
Action: Cluny, near Paris, sixteenth century.

A monk sells indulgences before the Cluny Abbey,
while peasants buy and sell. Jean, a young juggler, does his
juggling tricks and sings a song that the monk says offends
the Virgin. However, he will be pardoned if he joins the
brotherhood. Seeing the cook's donkey loaded with good
things to eat and drink, and being very hungry, Jean
agrees to become a monk. All the brethren, poets, painters,
etc., honor the Virgin with their arts, but poor Jean knows
only how to juggle and do tricks. So he decides to honor
the Virgin in his own way. When the monks find him
doing his tricks before the Virgin they are horrified and
are about to seize him when the cook cries, "Look!" The
statue of the Virgin is enveloped in a glorified light and
she stretches out her hands to bless the bewildered boy.
He dies of joy.

Pelleas and Melisande   Debussy
                                        (1862-1918)
Première: Paris, 1902.
Première: New York, Manhattan Opera House, 1908,
with Mary Garden as Melisande, Jean Perier as
Pelleas, Gerville-Reache as Genevieve, Hector
Dufranne as Golaud, Arimondi as Arkel.

94

Première: New York, Metropolitan Opera House,
    1925, with Lucrezia Bori as Melisande, Edward
    Johnson as Pelleas, Kathleen Howard as Gene-
    vieve, Clarence Whitehill as Golaud, Leon Rothier
    as Arkel.
Impressionistic tragic opera in five acts.
Book by Maeterlinck.
Action: The mystic medieval land of Allemonde.

Golaud, son of the blind King Arkel of the mystical
land of Allemonde, finds Melisande weeping beside a
spring in the forest. All she can remember is that she once
wore a crown. Golaud persuades her to become his bride.
This she does unwillingly. They are welcomed to the
castle by King Arkel, who forgives his son for marrying
an unknown maid, and by Pelleas, half-brother of Golaud.
Golaud neglects his young wife and she and Pelleas form
a warm friendship which ripens into love. Golaud's jealousy is aroused and he is cruel to Melisande. The lovers
meet at dusk and as they kiss, Golaud stabs Pelleas, while
Melisande flees to the castle. She bears Golaud's child but
he doubts her faithfulness. She denies his accusations but
says she loves Pelleas. The old King quiets his son while
Melisande passes quietly away.

La Reine Fiamette   Xavier Leroux
                                  (1863-1919)
Première: Paris, 1903.
Première: New York, Metropolitan Opera House,
    1919, with Farrar as the Queen, Adamo Didur as
    the Prince Consort, Leon Rothier as Cardinal
    Sforza, Hipolito Lazaro as Danielo.

95

French

Tragic opera in three acts.
Book by Mendes.
Action: Renaissance Kingdom of Bologna, fifteenth
century.

Cardinal Sforza wishes to be rid of Queen Fiamette and
makes Danielo promise that he will kill her. The Cardinal
has told Danielo that Fiamette has slain his (Danielo's)
brother. This is not true, but Danielo goes to Bologna to
kill Fiamette. He discovers that she is his beloved whom
he knows as Helene. She convinces him that she did not
kill his brother and Danielo tries to kill the Cardinal, at
whose command both Danielo and Queen Fiamette are
slain.

Ariane and Bluebeard   Paul Dukas
                                       (1865-1935)
Première: Paris, 1907.
Première: New York, Metropolitan Opera House,
        1910, with Farrar as Ariane, Leon Rothier as Blue-
        beard, Florence Wickham as the Nurse. Toscanini
        conducted.
Allegorical romantic opera in three acts.
Story after Perrault's fairy tale, *Bluebeard and His
        Seven Wives.* Book by Maeterlinck.
Action: A castle near a French village, medieval times.

Ariane becomes the wife of Bluebeard in spite of warn-
ings of the disappearance of five former wives. Accompanied by her nurse she goes to live at his castle. He gives
Ariane six silver keys and one golden key. She may use

96

the six silver keys but not the one of gold. Out of the six doors pour precious jewels. When she opens the seventh door with the golden key, human wails are heard and she discovers the five former wives. She leads them out into the sunshine and when they return to the castle they deck themselves in the jewels. Bluebeard is brought to the castle wounded. His wives care for him. Ariane binds up his wounds and she and her nurse leave. His other wives remain but Ariane goes out to claim freedom.

Le Chemineau	Leroux
(The Vagabond)	(1863-1919)

Première: Paris, 1907.
Première: New Orleans, 1911.
Première: Chicago, 1919, Chicago Opera Association, with Yvonne Gall as Toinette, Georges Baklanoff as Francois, Alfred Maguenat as the Vagabond, Myrna Sharlow as Aline, Octave Dua as Toinet, Gustave Huberdeau as Pierre.
Première: New York, 1919, Lexington Theatre, with same company.
Tragi-romantic opera in four acts.
Book by Jean Richepin.
Action: Provincial France.

Toinette, a farmer's daughter, loves the Vagabond, who has been working on her father's farm, and she refuses to marry the steady Francois. Having been betrayed by the Vagabond and hearing that he is preparing to leave, she tries to follow him but is persuaded by Francois not to do

97

French

so and to marry him. When the Vagabond's son, Toinet, is born, Francois thinks he is his son and rears him as such. Aline, daughter of a rich neighbor, Pierre, falls in love with Toinet, but her father knows something of Toinet's birth and will not consent. When Francois learns the truth he falls ill and is about to die when the Vagabond returns, begs forgiveness and promises to gain the consent of Pierre to the wedding of the young people. Francois dies, commending Toinette to the love of the Vagabond. He, however, feels the urge of the open and leaves again. Toinet and Aline are married and Toinette, now old and worn with grief mourns for the Vagabond.

La Habanera   Raoul Laparra
                                                (1876-   )

Première: Paris, 1908.
Première: Boston, 1910, (American Première) with
    Fely Dereyne as Pilar, Ramon Blanchart as Ramon,
    Jean Lasalle as Pedro.
Première: New York, Metropolitan Opera House,
        1924, with Florence Easton as Pilar, Armand
    Tokyatan as Pedro, Guiseppe Danise as Ramon.
Tragic opera in three acts.
Libretto by composer.
Action: Castile, Spain, present time.

Ramon loves Pilar who is to wed his brother Pedro. Pilar enters in her bridal costume to dance the Habanera with her promised husband but Ramon forces his brother into a quarrel and stabs Pedro in the back. Pedro, dying, tells Ramon that he will return in a year. Pilar faints when she finds Pedro dead, and Ramon, as though innocent, swears to avenge his brother's death. A year passes and Pedro's spirit appears among the dancers. Ramon, terrified, hears Pedro's voice telling him to confess. While Pilar is laying flowers on Pedro's grave Ramon hears the voice of his brother humming the Habanera. He sees Pilar lying on the grave, screams the truth in her ear, but she is dead. Ramon goes mad.

Monna Vanna   Fevrier
                                          (1875-   )
Première: Paris, 1909.
Première: Boston, 1913 (American Première), Boston
    Opera Company, with Mme. Georgette LeBlanc,
    wife of Maeterlinck, in the title role.
Première: Chicago, 1914 (first time) Chicago Grand
    Opera Company, with Mary Garden as Monna
    Vanna, Lucien Muratore as Prinzivalle, Vanni-
    Marcoux as Guido, Gustave Huberdeau as Marco.
Première: New York, Lexington Theatre, 1918, with
    same company.
Lyric drama in three acts.
Book by Maeterlinck.
Action: Pisa, Italy, end of fifteenth century.

   Guido Colonna is commander of the garrison at Pisa which is besieged by the Florentines under Prinzivalle. Prinzivalle agrees to raise the siege if Monna Vanna, wife of Guido, will come to his tent for the night. Guido refuses, but Monna Vanna is willing to sacrifice herself for her people. When she enters his tent, Prinzivalle sends food and supplies to Pisa. He reminds her of their childhood together and tells her that he has always loved her. Outwardly she remains loyal to her husband. When the word comes that Prinzivalle is to be arrested for sending food to the enemy, she persuades him to return with her to her husband's camp. Guido is consumed with jealousy in spite of her assurance that no harm has come to her, and throws Prinzivalle into a dungeon. Monna Vanna procures the key and frees him. Her love being awakened by the contrast between the two men she leaves with Prinzivalle for a life of happiness and freedom.

Quo Vadis?   Jean Nougues
                                                        (1876-   )

Première: Nice, 1909.
Première: Philadelphia, 1911 (American Première) by
    Philadelphia Chicago Opera Company with Alice
    Zipelli as Lygia, Lillian Grenville as Eunice, Maurice Renaud as Petronius, Dalmores as Vicinnius.
Première: New York, Metropolitan Opera House,
    1912, with same company and cast.
Tragic opera in five acts.
Book by Henri Cain, after the romance by Henry
    Sienkiewicz.
Action: Rome, first century of the Christian era.

Lygia, a Christian girl in a Roman household, will not yield her virtue to Vicinnius and is denounced by him. She is condemned to death in the arena but is rescued from the horns of the bull by her faithful attendant, Ursus. Later she marries Vicinnius who has become a Christian.

Don Quichotte	Massenet
	(1842-1912)

Première: Monte Carlo, 1910.

Première: New Orleans, 1912.

Première: Philadelphia, 1913, by Chicago Grand Opera Company with Mary Garden as Dulcinea, Vanni-Marcoux as the Don, Hector Dufranne as Sancho.

Première: New York, Metropolitan Opera House, 1926 (first time), with Florence Easton as Dulcinea, Feodor Chaliapin as the Don, Guiseppe de Luca as Sancho.

Serio-comic opera in five acts.

Book by Henri Cain. Story after the Spanish romance, *Don Quixote de la Mancha,* by Cervantes. Translated into a French drama by Jacques le Lorrain.

Action: Spain, in the middle ages.

A clever satire on the extravagant and exaggerated ideas of chivalry. The story deals with the various adventures and episodes in the life of gentle Don Quixote who thinks himself called to avenge the wrongs of the oppressed and underprivileged, his servant Sancho, and his lady-love, Dulcinea.

L'Heure Espagnole	Maurice Ravel
(Spanish Hour)	(1875-1937)

Première: Paris, 1911.

Première: Chicago, 1920 (American Première), with

Yvonne Gall as Concepcion, Alfred Maguenat as Ramiro.

Première: New York, Metropolitan Opera House,
1925 (first time), with Lucrezia Bori as Concepcion, Lawrence Tibbett as Ramiro.

Comic opera in one act.

Book by Franc Nohain.

Action: A clock shop in Toledo, Spain, eighteenth century.

Old Torquemada the clock-maker, is about to go out to regulate the public clocks of Toledo when Ramiro comes in to have his watch repaired. The clock-maker tells him to wait until he comes back. Concepcion, the young wife of the clock-maker, is expecting her lover and so wishes to be rid of Ramiro. Ramiro offers to carry a heavy clock, too heavy for her husband to lift, up-stairs for her. Gonzalve the lover comes and she hides him in a big grandfather's clock. Ramiro returns and carries the grandfather's clock to Concepcion's room. Inigo, a banker, comes in. He too is hidden in a clock. The husband returns and finds the rejected suitors hidden in his clocks. He laughs and so do all the others and they end up with a spirited quintette.

| *La Foret Bleue* | L. Francois Aubert |
| (The Blue Forest) | (1877-   ) |

Première: Boston, 1913, Boston Grand Opera Company, with Fernand De-Potter as Prince Charming, Jean Riddez as the Ogre, Carmen Melis as the

Princess, Jeska Swartz as Tom Thumb, Bernice Fisher as Red Riding-Hood, Elizabeth Amsden as the Fairy.
Fairy opera in three acts.
Book by Jacques Cheneviere. Story from old fairy tales.
Action: Fairy-land.

The story is a combination of episodes from the well-loved old fairy tales, Hop-O'-My-Thumb, Red Riding-Hood, and the Sleeping Beauty. Prince Charming falls in love with the Princess. He finds her later in her castle under the spell of sleep, from which he wakes her with a kiss. Fairy wedding-bells are heard and all ends happily.

Julien   Charpentier
                                                    (1860-   )
Première: Paris, 1913.
Première: New York, Metropolitan Opera House,
     1914, with Farrar as Louise, Caruso as Julien.
Tragic music drama in prologue and four acts.
Book by composer. Sequel to *Louise*.
Action: Paris or elsewhere. A tale of a poet's life. The
     thought of the poet of the present day may imagine
     its own environment.

Louise is dead. Julien is with her always in thought. He sees her as in a dream, as five different women, one by one, who descend lower and lower in the scale of life, ending in the gutter. In the last vision he is derided heartlessly by one who seems to have taken Louise's place, and he falls dead at her feet.

103

French

====

Marouf	Henri Rabaud
	(1873-)

Première: Paris, 1914.
Première: New York, Metropolitan Opera House,
    1917, with Frances Alda as the Sultan's daughter,
    Guiseppe de Luca as Marouf, Kathleen Howard as
    Fatima his wife, Leon Rothier as the Sultan, de
    Segurola as the Vizier, Thos. Chalmers as Ali.
Spectacular Oriental opera in five acts.
Book by Lucien Nepoty after the story *Aladdin and
    His Wonderful Lamp.*
Action: Cairo. Khaitan, "a city somewhere between
    China and Morocco."

Marouf, a cobbler of Cairo, has a wife, Fatima, who is
an undisciplined shrew. No matter how kind he is she
drags him into court and has him cruelly beaten. At last
he leaves Cairo with some sailors. A rich friend, Ali, an
old schoolmate, finds him and tells him to go into the
bazaar and pose as a rich man. He obeys and tells tales of
his fabulous wealth. The Sultan becomes interested and
offers his daughter in marriage. Marouf is delighted for
she is very beautiful. He tells her he is poor, but she loves
him. Marouf has announced that his caravans have been
delayed. The Sultan places his wealth at his disposal.
Marouf and the Princess decide to elope. On the plain
near by they ask a ploughman for food. The Princess
takes the plough which hits against a ring attached to a
great stone. Marouf tries to move the stone and the ring
comes off in his hand. The Princess polishes it, and being
a magic ring, a genii appears. Marouf orders a caravan.

The Sultan arrives to catch the runaways when, lo! the caravan appears — camels, mules laden with jewels, gold, etc. So all ends happily.

Les Quatre Journees	Alfred Bruneau
(The Four Days)	(1857-)

Première: Paris, 1916. Conducted by the composer.
Tragic pastoral opera in four acts.
Story after an idea of Emile Zola.
Action: France, Spring–Summer–Autumn–Winter.

Springtime — Jean and Babette are married, the Abbe Lazarre, Jean's uncle, blessing the union.

Summer — There is war. Jean, slightly wounded, is asked by an enemy (as he believes) for a drink. Jean crawls to him and finds that he is an Alsatian and the two become friends and comrades.

Autumn — Workers are gathering grapes. The Abbe is now a very old man and caresses Jean's young son. He succumbs to a weak spell and passes away.

Winter — The children of Jean and Babette are grown. The floods undermining the old farmhouse, all seek safety on the top floor. A boat comes by with room for all but two. Jean and Babette push all the children into the boat and remain together to the end.

105

French

Gismonda   Henri Fevrier
(1875-   )

Première: Chicago, 1919, Chicago Opera Association,
    with Mary Garden as Gismonda, Charles Fontaine
    as Almerio, Alfred Maguerrat as Zaccaria.
Première: New York, (first time) same year, Lexing-
    ton Theatre with same company.
Romantic opera in three acts.
Story after play by Sardou.
Action: Athens, middle ages.

The little son of the Duchess of Gismonda is the rightful heir to the Dukedom, but Zaccaria Franco wishes to
be Duke and has his friend Gregory push the little boy
into a tiger pit. The Duchess promises to marry the man
who rescues her son. Almerio, a young peasant, does so,
but as she cannot marry a peasant, Gismonda promises to
go to his hut for a night. Zacarria follows her there and Gismonda stabs him to death. Almerio claims that he is the
murderer. Gismonda sets aside class prejudice in the face
of such nobility of character and decides to marry
Almerio, after handing over to justice the wicked Gregory.
All ends happily.

The Blue Bird   Albert Wolff
(L'Oiseau Bleau)   (1884-   )

Première: New York, Metropolitan Opera House,
    1919, (World Première), with Raymonde Delau-

106

nois as Tyltyl, Mary Ellis as Mytyl, Florence
Easton as Mummy Tyl, Paolo Ananian as Daddy
Tyl, Leon Rothier as Time.
Symbolic fairy opera in four acts.
Text by Maeterlinck.
Action: Woodcutter's cottage. Land of Memory.
Palace of Night. Garden of Happiness. Kingdom
of the Future, etc.

On Christmas Eve a bright light wakens Tyltyl and
Mytyl, children of the woodcutter. The fairy Berylune
tells them to seek the Blue Bird of Happiness. She gives
Tyltyl a green cap which has a magic diamond which,
when turned, changes all things to beauty. By its magic
they bring to life the personalities of the familiar things of
their daily life, light, fire, water, sugar, bread, etc. They
visit the Land of Memory, where they find a bird, but it
is black and they let it go. They discover a garden of beautiful birds in the Palace of Night, but each one dies when
touched. They see the Garden of Happiness, and the Kingdom of the Future, where Father Time is sending babies
down to earth. Tyltyl's diamond makes all these adventures possible, but they return to their home without the
Blue Bird. Christmas morning they wake to find that their
own dove, which they are sending to a little sick friend,
is blue! The little friend comes in later, well and happy
but while the children play with the bird it escapes. Tyltyl
begs that any one finding their Blue Bird will return it to
them, as they will need the Spirit of Happiness every day.

NOTE: The composer conducted the Première performance and
Maeterlinck was present.

French

La Brebis Egaree	Darius Milhaud
(The Lost Sheep)	(1892-)

Première: Paris, 1923.
Impressionistic musical romance in three acts and
    twenty scenes.
Libretto by Francis Jammes.

The tale of a misguided young woman, wife of an honest
man, who, in a moment of passion goes off with a (supposed) friend of her husband's, with whom she finds nothing but misery and unhappiness. Full of repentance she
returns and begs to be taken back. Her husband forgives
and welcomes her back to his protecting care.

Judith	Arthur Honegger
	(1892-)

Première: Mezieres, Switzerland, 1925.
Première: Chicago, 1927 (American Première),
    Chicago Civic Opera Company, with Mary Gar-
    den as Judith, Caesare Formichi as Holofernes.
Tragic music drama in three acts. Libretto by Rene
    Morax. A modern score.
Story after the Biblical episode.

Bethulia is besieged by Holofernes, the arch-enemy of
the Jews, and commander of the Assyrians. Judith, a
beautiful Jewess, determines to save her people. She goes
to the tent of Holofernes and captivates him with her

charm and beauty. After a banquet given in her honor, at which she has drugged his wine, Holofernes sinks into a drunken stupor and Judith beheads him. She returns with his head to Bethulia and her townsmen fall upon the Assyrians and defeat them.

Le Pauvre Matelot	Milhaud
(The Poor Sailor)	(1892-)

Première: Paris, 1927, as *A Lament in three acts*.
Première: Philadelphia, 1937 (American Première), with Anna Leskaya as the Wife, Fritz Kreuger as the Sailor. Curtis Institute of Music.
Tragic opera in one act and three scenes, with English translation by Lorraine N. Finley.
Libretto by Jean Cocteau.

A sailor has not been heard from by his wife for fifteen years. In all this time she has kept his bar, looking forward to his return. She has refused offers of marriage, for she loves her husband and believes that he will return. One night there is a knock at the door. A stranger enters. It is her husband but she does not recognize him. He tells her that he knows her husband and that he is on his way home, but because of his debts he must travel by night so as to avoid the police. He shows her a valuable necklace (to try her faithfulness). She holds it for a moment and returns it to the stranger. He asks to stay the night and she prepares a bed for him. The idea comes to murder him and take the necklace to help her husband when he comes. While the sailor sleeps she kills him with a hammer.

109

XXth CENTURY OPERA
French

=====

Eros Vanqueur Pierre de Breville
(1861-   )

Première: Paris, 1932.
Lyric allegory in three acts and four scenes.
Libretto by Jean Lorrain.
Action: Illyria during the Italian Renaissance.

A king keeps his three lovely daughters imprisoned in his palace, being determined that they shall never come in contact with love nor experience its power. But Eros determines otherwise and, in disguise, gains entrance into the palace, and succeeds in getting two of the princesses, one at a time, to follow him. The third princess dies in her prison tower, rejoicing that at last she is free to love.

Maximilian Milhaud
(1892-   )

Première: Paris, 1932.
Tragic opera in three acts and nine scenes. Libretto by
    R. S. Hoffman and A. Lunel.
Story after the play, *Jaurez and Maximilian,* by Werfel.
Action: Mexico, 1865.

The story depicts the final struggle between Maximilian of Mexico and the rebel leader, Juarez. Maximilian is betrayed, captured and executed. Juarez, triumphant, is called by the people their Liberator.

| *La Femme Neu* | Fevrier |
| (The New Woman) | (1875-   ) |

Première: Paris, 1932.
Lyric drama in four acts. Libretto by Louis Payen.
Story after play by Henri Bataille.
Action: Paris, present time. Artist life.

Pierre Bernier, an artist, wins the Medal of Honor at the Salon for his successful painting, *La Femme Neu*. He wishes his model, Luette, to share his success and asks her to marry him. They live happily for a few years, when he becomes enamored of the lovely Princess de Chabran, the young wife of a degenerate old Prince. The Prince thinks he can secure profit from Pierre by divorcing his wife. Luette attempts suicide, and her husband, becoming remorseful, declares he will give up the Princess. A former lover of Luette's offers her his faithful love which has never changed in all the years and she accepts him.

| *Rolande et le Mauvais Garcon* | Rabaud |
| (Roland and the Rascal) | (1873-   ) |

Première: Paris, 1934.
Romantic opera in five acts. Libretto by Lucien Nepoty.
Action: An imaginary kingdom near the Mediterranean, Medieval times.

In an imaginary kingdom a young Queen lives in her enchanted gardens with no thought but of her own beauty

and goodness. Her royal husband has made his wife famous
through his writings, for he is a poet as well as a King.
One day she meets a "mauvais garcon," an adventurer,
full of wit. They are attracted to each other. The angry
King wishes to punish them and does so, — by a haughty
pardon! The couple immediately become tired of each
other, there being no further "adventure." The "mauvais
garcon" leaves the country and the Queen goes back to
her throne and her gardens.

Gargantua   Antoine Mariotte
                                                (1875-   )
Première: Paris, 1935.
Comic opera in three acts. Libretto by composer in
    collaboration with the poet, Armory.
    Story adapted from the Rabelaisian text.
Action: Imaginary episodes, sixteenth century.

Gargantua is a fantastic character who, from a preco-
cious infant, becomes a veritable giant. He makes war on
Picrochole and his followers and wins. Picrochole and two
of his captains are to be hung but Gargantua frees them.
All episodes are satirical and highly imaginary.

Merchant of Venice   Reynaldo Hahn
                                                (1874-   )
Première: Paris, 1935.
Comedy opera in three acts and five scenes.
Libretto by Miguel, in French verse, from Shake-
    speare's play.

AT HOME AND ABROAD
French

"The most notable feature of his new opera is the great respect with which Hahn has treated the text. . . . He closes the opera with a conventionally effective septet — sung by the three happy couples and the merchant Antonio — in which it is proclaimed that love must always have the final word."

(Gilbert Chase in Musical America,
April 25, 1935).

Oedipus   Georges Enesco
                                      (1881-   )

Première: Paris, 1936.
Lyrical tragedy in four acts and six tableaux.
Libretto by Edmond Flegg. Story follows the episodes
    in Greek mythology but differs slightly from
    Sophocles' dramatization.

In the palace of Laius at Thebes there is great rejoicing over the birth of a son. The mother (Jocasta) is about to name her son (Oedipus) when a blind soothsayer prophesies his terrible destiny. He will become the "assassin of his father and the husband of his mother." The babe is immediately sent away with a shepherd to be killed, but instead of killing the child the shepherd substitutes him for the dead child of one of his fellow shepherds. When he attains manhood Oedipus learns his destiny from an oracle and leaves Corinth. On the road he kills a man who assails him, not knowing that it was his own father. He reaches the gate of Thebes, where the Sphinx devours all who cannot answer her questions. The Thebans have de-

French

clared that any one who rids the city of this monster shall be King. Oedipus answers the questions, the Sphinx disappears, he is made King, and is received by Queen Jocasta, whom he marries. Years pass. When he learns that the man he killed on the road was his father, and the Queen (his wife) is his mother, he tears out his eyes and the Thebans send him into exile. His faithful daughter, Antigone, follows him in his wanderings. He finally gains peace of mind, bids farewell to his daughter, and dies.

Ninety-three   Charles Silver
                                                  (1868-   )

Première: Paris, 1936.
Tragic opera in three (or four) acts. Libretto by Henri
    Cain. Story based on Victor Hugo's novel.
Action: Time of the Vendean rebellion, immediately
    following the French Revolution in 1793.

Marquis de Lantenac of the nobility is in sympathy with the peasants and is the soul of the rebellion. Young Gouvain, an idealist and nephew to the Marquis, supports the Republic. La Houzarde is a jolly canteen woman, and La Flecharde, the mother of three children who are torn from her arms and taken as hostages. Cimourdain is a stern defender of the law and is devoted to Gouvain, whose execution has been ordered. Cimourdain, into whose hands the execution has been placed, shoots himself rather than put his beloved charge to death.

114

Esther de Carpentras   Milhaud
(1892-   )

Première: Paris, 1938.
Opera bouffe in two acts.
Story patterned somewhat after the Biblical story of
    Esther, with changes to suit the composer's oper-
    atic intentions.
Action: Carpentras in the Midi of France. Reign of
    Louis XV.

The yearly pageant commemorating the liberation of
the Hebrews by the beautiful Esther, from the wrath of
Ahasuerus, is taking place in Carpentras, at the time of the
reign of Louis XV. Permission for the pageant has been
obtained from the Cardinal. During the pageant the Cardinal appears in regal pomp and tells the Jews they must
choose between baptism into the Christian faith or ban-
ishment. Esther entreats the Cardinal, instead of the
Ahasuerus of the pageant, for clemency for her people.
This is granted and all join in a chorus, uniting for the
time, the voices of the Old and the New Testaments.

FRENCH OPERA

(PART II)

composed *before 1900*

and presented *for the first time*

in the United States during the

*XX*TH *Century*

(in prominent Opera Houses), also

Outstanding Revivals in the United

States during the same period

1900 — Season 1937–1938

(inclusive)

Salammbo   Ernest Reyer
                                                  (1823-1909)
Première: Brussels, 1890.
Première: New Orleans, 1900.
Première: New York, Metropolitan Opera House,
    1901, with Lucienne Breval as Salammbo, Albert
    Saleza as Matho, Carrie Bridewell as the Goddess
    Tanit, Antonio Scotti as Hamilcar.
Tragic opera in four acts.
Book by deLock. Story after Flaubert.
Action: Carthage, about 200 B. C.

  Matho, leader of the revolting Carthaginian mercenaries,
insists on marriage with Salammbo, daughter of Hamilcar
in whose gardens the soldiers are revelling. Salammbo re-
bukes their behavior and is about to wrap herself in the
holy veil of the Goddess Tanit when Matho snatches the
veil from her, wraps it about himself and escapes. Salammbo is commissioned to recover the veil. She does so through
pretended love of Matho and the veil is returned to the
temple. Hamilcar has defeated the rebels and Matho is
captured and condemned to be the human sacrifice for
Moloch. Salammbo is to kill him with her own hand. She
has fallen in love with him, however, and rather than
take his life she stabs herself. Matho catches her as she
falls to the ground and he falls on his sword.

Les Contes d'Hoffmann   Offenbach
   (Tales of Hoffmann)   (1819-1880)
Première: Paris, 1881.
Première: New York, 1882 (American Première),
    Fifth Avenue Theatre.

117

French

Première: New York, Manhattan Opera House, 1907, with Alice Zepilli as Olympia, Jeanne Jomelli as Giulietta, Camille Borello as Antonia, Maurice Renaud in the triple role, Coppelius, Dappertutto, Dr. Miracle, Charles Dalmores in the title rôle.

Première: New York, Metropolitan Opera House, for the first time, 1913, with Frieda Hempel as Olympia, Olive Fremstad as Giulietta, Lucrezia Bori as Antonia, Umberto Macnez as Hoffmann, Adamo Didur as Coppelius, Dinh Gilly as Dappertutto, Leon Rothier as Dr. Miracle.

Fantastic opera with prologue, three acts and epilogue. Story after one of A. E. T. Hoffmann's *Strange Tales*. Action: Nuremburg; Venice; Munich.

Prologue — Nuremburg. Hoffmann, the popular student, is carousing with companions in a wine cellar. He tells his experiences with three loves.

One of them, Olympia, proves to be a mechanical doll. After he has fallen in love with her and danced with her the mechanism runs down and "she" is smashed by her maker.

Venice — Giulietta is a courtesan who leads him to a duel with another of her lovers. Hoffmann kills his foe and flees for his life.

Munich — Antonia, his singing love, is told she must sing no more for death will be the penalty. The devil (Dr. Miracle) makes her sing. She dies.

Epilogue — Again the tavern in Nuremburg. Hoffmann is overcome by his emotions over the telling of his story.

Thais   Massenet
                                              (1842-1912)

Première: Paris, 1894.
Première: New York, Manhattan Opera House, 1908
    (American Première), with Mary Garden as
    Thais, Maurice Renaud as Athanael.
Première: New York, Metropolitan Opera House,
    1917, with Farrar as Thais, Amato as Athanael.
Tragic opera in three acts. Text by Gallet, after the
    novel by Anatole France.
Action: Alexandria; Egyptian desert; early Christian
    era.

Athanael, a young monk, lives in the desert. Learning
of the wicked Thais, the scandal of Alexandria, the town
of his birth, he hurries there to save the beautiful young
sinner. He finally persuades her to go to the desert, where
he places her in charge of the holy nuns. She is converted,
but Athanael has become infatuated with her. He goes to
the convent and finds her dying. He begs her to live and
love him but she points him heavenward. When she dies he
falls unconscious.

Armide   Gluck
                                              (1714-1787)

Première: Paris, 1777.
Première: New York, Metropolitan Opera House,
    1910 (American Première), with Fremstad as
    Armide, Caruso as Renaud, Amato as Hidraot,
    Louise Homer as La Haine.

Tragic opera in five acts. Text by P. Quinault.
Book after Tasso's *Jerusalem Delivered*.
Action: Damascus, time of the Crusades.

Renaud, a Christian Knight, is enticed by the beautiful pagan sorceress, Armide, and yields to her charms. Two of his Crusader companions endeavor to free him from her spell, but in vain. Ubald, one of the Knights, shows Renaud himself in a polished shield, as he was and as he is. He sees the light, rushes off and returns to his holy work. Armide uses every art to make him return to her but without success. In despair she perishes in the ruins of her castle which burns to the ground.

NOTE: Toscanini conducted the American première.

The Attack on the Mill	Alfred Bruneau
(L'Attaque du Moulin)	(1857-)

Première: Paris, 1893.
Première: New York, Metropolitan Opera Company, 1910, at the New Theatre, with Jane Noria as Franchette, Edmond Clement as Dominie, Dihn Gilly as the Miller.
Tragic opera in four acts.
Story after Emile Zola.
Action: France. War episode of 1870.

Franchette, the miller's daughter and young Dominie are to be married, when he is called to war. Later when

Dominie is warding off an attack of the Prussians on the mill, he is captured but is promised freedom if he will turn traitor. This he refuses to do. Franchette assists him to escape. He kills a sentry and hides. When the miller refuses to divulge the hiding-place of Dominie, he is ordered shot instead of Dominie. French soldiers come to the rescue, but too late to prevent the execution of the miller.

Les Pecheurs de Perles	Bizet
(Pearl Fishers)	(1838-1875)

Première: Paris, 1863.
Première: Philadelphia, 1893. United States Première.
Première: New York, Metropolitan Opera House,
    1896, two acts given.
Première: New York, Metropolitan Opera House,
    first time in its entirety, 1916, with Frieda Hempel
    as Leila, Caruso as Nadir, Guiseppe de Luca as
    Zirga, Leon Rothier as the High Priest.
Oriental opera in three acts. Libretto by Carre and
    Cormon.
Action: Ceylon. Legendary times.

Before the pearl fishers start on their dangerous work they appoint a vestal virgin to sing on the shore and ward off the evil spirits. Leila is chosen. Zinga, the chief, and his friend Nadir recognize her as the girl they had both loved at sight upon seeing her in a mosque. At that time

French

in order to prevent rivalry between them, they had left the place. Nadir and Leila, gazing at each other realize they are deeply in love. The fishermen of the clan are furious that the vestal virgin should be so tempted and they condemn her to death with Nadir. Zinga helps them to escape and perishes a victim of the wrath of the islanders.

Iphigenie en Tauride   Gluck
                                         (1714-1787)

Première: Paris, 1779.
Première: New York, Metropolitan Opera House,
      1916, with Melanie Kurt as Iphigenie, Hermann
      Weil as Orestes, Johannes Sembach as Pylades,
      Karl Braun as King Thoas.
Lyric drama in three acts.
Action: Tauris; Scythia, mythological times.

Iphigenie is serving in the temple of Artemis in Tauride, the wild land of Scythia. The King, Thoas, demands a human sacrifice. Two castaways are found on the shore and brought to the altar. Iphigenie recognizes one of them as her brother, Orestes, who has fled from Greece after killing his mother for murdering his father. The other, Pylades, she sends for help. When the Scythian King insists on sacrificing Orestes, Pylades returns with help and Orestes is saved. Iphigenie, her priestesses, her brother and his friend return to Greece, leaving Tauris forever.

| *La Juive* | Jacques Halevy |
| (The Jewess) | (1799-1862) |

Première: Paris, 1835.
Première: New Orleans, 1844. American Première.
Première: New York, Metropolitan Opera House,
1885. Many times after that. Notable revival at
the Metropolitan 1919, with Caruso as Eleazar,
Rosa Ponselle as Rachel, Orville Harrold as Leo-
pold, Leon Rothier as Cardinal Brogni, Evelyn
Scotney as Eudoxia.
Tragic opera in five acts.
Book by Scribe.
Action: Constance, 1414.

When Cardinal Brogni was a plain citizen he persecuted
the Jews and had two of the sons of Eleazar burned as
heretics. Later, Eleazar stole Brogni's baby daughter,
named her Rachel and brought her up as his own daughter and a Jewess. Years pass. Brogni is now a Cardinal and
Eleazar the wealthy goldsmith, who keeps busy in his
workshop and does not heed the ceremonies being held
in the Cathedral near by, to celebrate the victory over the
Hussites. The people, enraged at him, drag Eleazar and
his daughter into the street, but no harm comes to them because Cardinal Brogni intervenes. Prince Leopold falls in
love with Rachel and, disguised as a Jew, wins her love.
Rachel comes to the Town Hall to deliver a jewel to
Eudoxia, the bride of Leopold. She recognizes Leopold
and cries out that he is in love with her, a Jewess! The
Cardinal has Leopold, Eleazar and Rachel imprisoned.

123

They are condemned to die but Rachel intervenes and saves Leopold from death. She and Eleazar may become Christians, or die. They prefer death. When Rachel is thrown into the boiling oil, Eleazar cries to the Cardinal, "She was your daughter!" and himself plunges into the cauldron.

NOTE: Caruso's last operatic appearance was on Christmas Eve of 1920, in *La Juive*. He was taken ill the next day, indeed was suffering at the time of the performance, from the illness which finally resulted in his death in Naples, in August, 1921. Eleazar was one of his outstanding parts and his appearance in that character never failed to thrill the audience.

Le Roi d'Ys   Eduard Lalo
                                                 (1823-1893)
Première: Paris, 1888.
Première: New Orleans, 1890. American Première.
Première: New York, (first time) Metropolitan Opera House, 1922, with Frances Alda as Rozenn, Rosa Ponselle as Margared, Beniamino Gigli as Mylio, Giuseppe Danise as Karnac, Leon Rothier as the King.
Tragic opera in three acts and five scenes.
Text by E. Blau, based on an old legend about the flooding of the ancient city of Ys.
Action: Ancient Brittany, middle ages.

Margared, daughter of the King of Ys, is to marry Karnac and thus bring peace, for he is a foe feared by all. Rozenn, sister of Margared, secretly loves Mylio, who is off at the war. Margared secretly loves Mylio also and

124

when he returns on her wedding day she refuses to marry Karnac who immediately declares war. Mylio goes out to fight and Margared is in a fury when she discovers that Mylio loves Rozenn. She conspires with Prince Karnac, who has been defeated, and they plan to open the sluice gates which protect the city from the sea. Mylio and Rozenn are returning from their wedding when they see the raging waters and flee with the King to a high spot. Margared feels remorse and praying for the safety of the city she throws herself into the flood. The waters quiet down and all are saved except Margared, who perishes.

La Vestale   Gasparo Spontini
                                               (1774-1851)

Première: Paris, 1807.
Première: Philadelphia, 1828, by a French Opera Company of New Orleans.
Première: New York, (first time), Metropolitan Opera House, 1925, with Rosa Ponselle as Julia, Margaret Matzenauer as the Chief Vestal, Edward Johnson as Licinius, Jose Mardones as the High Priest, de Luca as Cinna.
Near-tragic opera in three acts.
Text by DeJuoy.
Action: Ancient Rome.

Julia is betrothed to Licinius. During his absence at the wars she becomes a vestal virgin. This compels her to renounce mortal love, and upon his return she regrets her hasty action. As they meet in the temple, in an abandon

125

of love and despair, Julia allows the sacred fire on the altar to go out. This is a sacrilege for which she is condemned to be buried alive. Licinius is saved by his friend, Cinna, and pleads in vain for Julia's pardon. As she descends into her living tomb, a lightning bolt from the Goddess Vesta rekindles the sacred altar flame and Julia is forgiven. The High Priest unites the two lovers amidst great rejoicing.

Iphigenie en Aulide   Gluck
                                          (1714-1787)

Première: Paris, 1774.
Première: Philadelphia, 1935, with George Baklanoff as Agamemnon, Cyrena van Gordon as Clytemnestra, Rose Teutoni as Iphigenia, Joseph Bentonelli as Achilles.
Lyric drama in three acts.
Book after Racine's play. Libretto by Du Rollet.
Action: Aulis; Troy; Rome. Legendary period of the epic figures of Euripidean drama.

Into Aulis Harbor the Greek fleet cannot sail as there is no wind, and the soothsayer tells Agamemnon that if he will sacrifice his daughter, Iphigenie, to the Goddess Artemis, the winds will blow. Iphigenie is willing, but her betrothed, Achilles, remonstrates with the King. The people clamor for the sacrifice. A storm arises and the Goddess Artemis appears, declares that the noble loyalty of Iphigenie has saved her from death and no sacrifice is demanded. The lovers are united amid songs of joy.

126

GERMAN OPERA

(PART I)

composed and presented abroad,

in the United States, or in both, during the

XXTH *Century*

1900 — Season 1937–1938

(inclusive)

Character of German Opera

Italian influence in German opera developed a love for music itself. With the entrance of Carl Maria von Weber's epoch-making *Der Freischütz*, with its fine orchestration, harmonic invention, scenic effects and dramatic action, he was acclaimed the Founder of German National Opera.

127

German

The Polish Jew   Karel Weiss
                                                  (1862-   )
Première: Prague, 1901.
Première: New York, Metropolitan Opera House,
      1921, with Chief Caupolican as Mathis, William
      Gustafson as The Jew, Raymonde Delaunois as
      Annette, Mario Chamlee as Christian, Kathleen
      Howard as the wife of Mathis.
Tragic opera in two acts.
Text by Ruchard Batka and Victor Leon.
Action: An Alsatian village, 1833.

  Mathis, burgomaster and innkeeper of Alsatia, one
winter night murders a Polish Jew for his money. He is
haunted with the memory. Fifteen years pass. Annette, his
daughter, and Christian are celebrating their approaching
marriage when a Polish Jew, similar in looks and actions
to the murdered man, appears in their midst. Mathis, horrified, collapses and is carried to his bed. Later when his
wife goes to waken him she finds him dead. In a night-
mare he has believed himself tried at court and sentenced
to death for the murder and in his fright has died in his
sleep.

Tiefland   D'Albert
                                                  (1864-1932)
Première: Prague, 1903.
Première: New York, Metropolitan Opera House,
      1908, with Emmy Destinn as Martha, Fritz Fein-
      hals as Sebastino, Eric Schmedes as Pedro.

Music drama with prologue and three acts.

Libretto by Lothar. Story after a Spanish tragedy by Guimera.

Action: The Pyrenees and the valley of Catalonia.

Sebastino, a lowland farmer, has betrayed Martha, an innocent and helpless girl, and now wishes to be rid of her so that he may marry a rich widow. He plans to have Pedro, a good young shepherd boy, marry Martha and brings him to the lowland mill and tells Martha she must marry Pedro and that he, Sebastino, will visit her on her wedding night. Pedro and Martha are married and Pedro gives her his little store of silver and tells her that he is so happy that his dream of a pure young wife has come true. She is dismayed and spends the night with Pedro at her feet, so Sebastino does not dare enter. She tells Pedro her sad story but not the name of her betrayer. The rich widow refuses Sebastino and he comes to Martha, who in terror calls Pedro. Pedro strangles Sebastino and takes Martha back with him to his mountain home there to live a pure and peaceful life together.

Salome   Richard Strauss
                                                  (1864-1905)

Première: Dresden, 1905.

Première: New York, Metropolitan Opera House,
        1907, with Olive Fremstad as Salome, Marion
        Weed as Herodias, Carl Burrian as Herod, Anton
        Rooy as John, Andreas Dippel as Narraboth. One

performance. The Board of Directors forbade a repetition as "objectionable to the interest of the Metropolitan Opera House."

Première: New York, 1909, Hammerstein produced it successfully at his Manhattan Opera House, in French, with Mary Garden as Salome, Augusta Doria as Herodias, Charles Dalmores as Herod, Hector Dufranne as John.

Tragic music drama in one act.

After the play by Oscar Wilde. Founded on the Biblical story.

Action: Tiberias, Galilee, 30 A. D.

Narraboth, Captain of King Herod's guard, loves Salome, but she is tired of familiar vices and yearns for some novel experience. The voice of John the Baptist from his cistern prison attracts her and she persuades Narraboth to bring John to her. She is shameless in her wooing of the prophet and Narraboth, mad with jealousy, kills himself, while John curses her and returns to his prison. Herod and his courtiers, all intoxicated, come to the terrace and Salome dances before them. As a reward, she asks the head of John the Baptist brought to her. He is beheaded, and when she kisses his dead lips, Herod, base as he is, shudders and cries, "Kill this woman!" She is crushed to death by his guards.

NOTE: The once sinful Salome was given at the Metropolitan Opera House again on January 13, 1934, with a highly successful performance in which the Salome was Gota Ljungberg, Dorothee Manski sang Herodias, Max Lorenz, Herod, and Friedrich Schorr was the John.

Electra   Richard Strauss
                                             (1864-1905)

Première: Dresden, 1909.

Première: New York, Manhattan Opera House, 1910,
   (in French), with Madame Mazarin as Electra,
   Gerville-Reache as Clytemnestra, Gustave Huberdeau as Orestes, Jean Duffault as Aegisthus.

Première: First time at Metropolitan Opera House,
   1932 (in German) with Gertrude Kappel as Electra, Gota Ljungberg as Clytemnestra, Friedrich
   Schorr as Orestes, Rudolf Laubenthal as Aegisthus.

Tragic music drama in one act.

Text by Hofmannstahl. Mythical tale of ancient
   Greece (After Sophocles).

   Agamemnon has been murdered by his wife, Clytemnestra and her paramour, Aegisthus. His daughter, Electra,
determines to avenge his death and so tells her mother,
who is now full of remorse, what to expect. When Orestes,
her brother, returns she gives him the axe with which
Agamemnon was killed and tells him their mother, Clytemnestra, must die in like manner. The death shriek is heard.
Aegisthus, unsuspecting, approaches and Electra holds the
torch that he may enter. He meets his death in turn with
the same axe. Electra dances herself into a frenzy and
falls unconscious.

Königskinder   Engelbert Humperdinck
(King's Children)   (1854-1921)

Première: New York, Metropolitan Opera House,
   1910, with Geraldine Farrar as the Goose-Girl,

Herman Jadlowker as the King's Son, Louise Homer as the Witch, Otto Goritz as the Fiddler. This was the World Première of the Opera — the composer present.
Allegorical fairy opera in three acts.
Book by Elsa Bernstein.
Action: Hellabrunn, in the mountains of Germany, middle ages.

The Goose-Girl with her geese is seen by the King's Son before the witch's hut. He falls in love with her and begs her to become his Queen, but the witch's magic spell keeps her from fleeing with him. Thinking she is cowardly he tells her he will not return until a star falls from the sky and the lily buds before the hut bloom. At noon on a certain day, predicts the witch, the first person who comes through the town gate will be their King. The day comes. A star falls from the sky and the lilies bloom. The King's Son comes through the gate, where the Goose-Girl stands. He falls at her feet and acclaims her his Queen. But the people will not accept them, are incensed, and drive the Royal Children out. Happily and hand-in-hand they go but are lost in the woods. Cold and hungry they come to the Witch's hut. The King's Son gives his crown for a loaf of bread. The bread has been poisoned. They share it and die together.

Der Rosenkavalier
(Cavalier of the Rose)

Richard Strauss
(1864-1905)

Première: Dresden, 1911.
Première: New York, Metropolitan Opera House,

1913, with Marguerite Ober as Octavian, Frieda Hempel as the Princess, Anna Case as Sophie, Otto Goritz as Baron Ochs.

Comedy opera in three acts.

Text by von Hofmannstahl.

Action: Vienna, time of Empress Maria Theresa, eighteenth century.

Octavian, a youth of noble birth, is in the room of the Princess, whose husband is away at the hunt. When about to be discovered, he dons a maid's dress and hides, as the Baron Ochs, a distant cousin of the Princess enters. He wants the Princess to name a Cavalier of the Rose who will, as his proxy, present the traditional silver betrothal rose to his fiance, the lovely convent-bred Sophie. The Princess suggests Octavian and he and Sophie fall in love at first sight. The Baron has begun a flirtation with the maid (Octavian) and after a series of amusing incidents the Princess succeeds in smoothing the path of the young lovers, Octavian and Sophie, and they are united, much to the chagrin of the Baron.

Ariadne in Naxos   Richard Strauss
                                     (1864-1905)

Première: Stuttgart, 1912.

Première: Philadelphia, (American Première), 1928 (in German) with Alma Peterson as Ariadne, Charlotte Boykin as Zerbinetta, Judson House as Bacchus, Nelson Eddy in double role of Wigmaker and Harlequin, Helen Jepson as Echo (her operatic debut).

German

Première: First time in New York, Juilliard Opera
School, 1934, in English, with Martha Dwyer as
Ariadne, Josephine Antoine as Zerbinetta, Albert
Gifford as Bacchus.
Lyric drama with prologue and two acts.
Book by von Hofmannstahl. Story in part from Mo-
liere's comedy *Le Bourgeois gentilhomme.* An
opera within an opera.
Action: Vienna, eighteenth century.

A rich music lover of Vienna is presenting in his private
theatre an opera by a young composer. A dancing troupe,
headed by Zerbinetta, has also been invited to entertain
and the young Venetian decides to combine the two,
tragedy and comedy. So when Ariadne has been deserted
by Theseus for her sister, Phaedra, and the island is filled
with her cries for death, Zerbinetta and her companions
try to console her with joyous entertainment, but without
success. Bacchus appears, Ariadne sinks into his arms. New
life and joy have come to her instead of death and the end
is happiness.

Mona Lisa   Max von Schillings
(1868-1933)
Première: Stuttgart, 1915.
Première: New York, Metropolitan Opera House,
1923, with Barbara Kemp (wife of the composer)
as Mona Lisa, Michael Bohnen as Francesco del
Gioconda, Curt Taucher as Giovanni. In the pro-

logue and the epilogue, Barbara Kemp as the Wife,
Michael Bohnen as the Husband, Curt Taucher as
the Lay Brother.

Tragic opera with prologue, two acts, and epilogue.
Libretto by Beatrice Dovsky.

Action: Prologue and epilogue in the twentieth century. Acts one and two, in the time of the Renaissance. The place is Florence.

Prologue — The twentieth century. A tourist and his
much younger wife visit a monastery which was once the
home of the pearl merchant, Francesco del Gioconda, during the Renaissance, about 1498. The lay brother who is
their guide tells the story:

Francesco, aged husband of Mona Lisa, is a pearl
merchant. Giovanni, envoy of the Pope, comes to buy a
precious pearl. The house is filled with guests and Francesco opens the doors of his jewel-closet (just large enough
for one man, and air-tight) and shows them how he draws
the pearl casket up from the waters of the river beneath,
which keeps the gems perfect. Mona Lisa, as is her custom,
takes the Pope's pearl to warm it in her breast and Giovanni recognizes in her his long lost love, who disappeared
while he was absent from Rome. (Mona Lisa had been
forced by her parents to marry the aged Francesco.)
When the guests leave, Giovanni remains and Mona Lisa
agrees to flee with him. Francesco creeps in and sees them
in each other's arms, creeps out and enters noisily. Mona
Lisa has pushed Giovanni into the jewel-closet. Francesco
carelessly locks the closet and throws the key into the
river. Next day, Dianora, the step-daughter, finds the key

135

in a boat and gives it to Mona Lisa, who, knowing that Giovanni is dead, gives it to Francesco. He opens the closet and enters it. Mona Lisa pushes the door shut, locks it and then goes to church to seek repentance.

Epilogue — The same as the Prologue. The story is finished. The tourists leave, but as she goes, the young wife gives her flowers and some mass money to the young lay brother. Here is the same situation as in the story, but in the twentieth century. As the Brother sees the wife follow her husband away from the monastery he cries after her, "Mona Lisa, Mona Lisa!"

Violanta   Eric Korngold
                                               (1897-   )
Première: Munich, 1916.
Première: New York, Metropolitan Opera House,
        1927, with Jeritza as Violanta, Whitehill as Simone
        Trevais, Kirschhoff as Alfonso.
Tragic opera in one act.
Text by Hans Muller. A Renaissance tragedy.
Action: Venice, fifteenth century.

Violanta, wife of Simone Trovais, determines to avenge the shame and death of her sister, Nerina, and lays plans to kill Don Alfonso, the seducer. Her husband agrees to assist her and allows her to invite Alfonso to their home. When Simone hears her sing a song, he is to stab Alfonso. Alfonso arrives and makes violent love to Violanta who realizes that she loves him. Unconsciously, in her happiness, she begins to sing and Simone rushes in and witnesses their embraces and hears his wife declare her love for Alfonso. He thrusts the dagger at Alfonso, but Violanta throws herself between them and receives the stab in her breast. As she dies she thanks Simone for saving her honor.

NOTE: This opera was composed when Korngold was but seventeen years of age and is in modern style.

| *The Woman Without a Shadow* | Richard Strauss |
| (Childless Woman) | (1864-1905) |

Première: Vienna, 1919.
Symbolic opera in three acts.
Libretto by von Hoffmannstahl.

An Eastern Emperor has married a Fairy Princess who is childless. The Emperor will turn to stone if the Empress has no "shadow." Her Nurse tries to persuade the young wife of a dyer to exchange her shadow for gold, but the Empress refuses to take the shadow because of the unhappiness it causes the dyer and his wife, who have become separated and are blindly searching for each other. The Emperor is beginning to turn to stone. The Empress visits a temple and voices bid her drink of the water that will pass to her the "shadow" of the dyer's wife, but she refuses to gain happiness through another's suffering. The Emperor becomes stone, but the Empress still refuses to drink. Suddenly she realizes that she has a shadow of her own. Her unselfishness has been rewarded and the Emperor is restored.

137

German

The Revolutionary Wedding   Eugen D'Albert
  (Die Revolutionshochzeit)   (1864-1932)

Première: Berlin, 1919.
Tragic opera in three acts.
Story after the drama by Sophie Michaelis.
Action: France at the time of the Revolution, 1793.

Ernest, a young Royalist officer, has just married Alaine, when he is captured by Marc-Arron, an officer of the Revolution. Ernest is condemned to death, but is allowed a respite until six o'clock the next morning. Alaine secures his liberty with herself as the price, Marc-Arran having fallen in love with her.

   The Dead City   Korngold
  (Die Todt Stadt)   (1897-   )

Première: Vienna, 1920. Hamburg and Cologne in the
    same year.
Première: New York, Metropolitan Opera House,
    1921, with Jeritza (her American debut) as Mari-
    etta, Orville Harrold as Paul.
Visionary opera in three acts. Book by Paul Schott.
Story after Rodenbach's drama, *Le Mirage*, from his
    novel, *Bruges la mort*.
Action: Bruges, nineteenth century.

For years Paul has mourned the death of his wife, Marie. Her picture is on the wall and a long braid of her golden

138

hair is in a glass case in the room. He meets a woman, Marietta, a dancer, who is the counterpart of his dead wife. She becomes his mistress but is never permitted to enter his house, which is sacred to his wife. When the infatuation is beginning to wear off she comes to his home. When she leaves, Paul has a dream in which Marietta taunts the picture of Marie, seizes the braid of Marie's hair, and dances wildly around the room. Paul in remorse and horror, curses her and strangles her with the braid of hair. When he awakes he is alone. Marietta returns for her parasol and the roses which he has given her. She would stay, but Paul is indifferent, and she leaves.

Wozzeck   Alban Berg
                                  (1885-1935)
Première: Berlin, 1925.
Première: Philadelphia, 1931. (American première), with Anna Roselle as Marie, Ivan Ivantzoff as Wozzeck, Gabriel Leonoff as the Drum Major.
Première: New York, Metropolitan Opera House, 1931, by the Philadelphia Grand Opera Company with the same cast except the Drum Major, which was sung by Nelson Eddy.
Modernistic tragic opera in three acts of five scenes each. A musical development of a drama by Georg Buechner. Berg formed the libretto into three parts: Exposition, Denouement, Catastrophe.

Wozzeck, a daily toiler of ordinary intelligence and easily crushed by those in power, discovers that his vicious,

German

weak wife, Marie, is in love with a pompous drum major, who jeers at the poor Wozzeck. So goaded is he that he determines to murder his wife. This he does and then kills himself.

Note: The Philadelphia performance was in March, the Metropolitan in November, of 1931.

Egyptian Helen   Richard Strauss
                                                   (1864-1905)
Première: Dresden, 1928.
Première: New York, Metropolitan Opera House,
    1928, with Rethberg as Helen, Laubenthal as
    Menelaus, Whitehill as Shiek Alter, Edith Fleisch-
    er as Aithra the sorceress.
Spectacular opera in three acts.
Action: Troy; fairy palace of Aithra the sorceress; oasis in African desert, mythological times.

Helen, beautiful wife of King Menelaus, is carried off by Paris, the Trojan guest of the King, and war between the Greeks and Trojans results. The victorious Greeks restore Helen to her husband, who, filled with hate and jealousy, would kill her. Their ship is wrecked and the pair come to the castle of the sorceress Aithra. She mixes a magic potion to be given Menelaus to destroy all memory of Helen's infidelity and they go to Egypt to begin a new life. Helen becomes tired of keeping her husband under the spell of the magic potion, and throws it away, depending on winning him back by her own charm, in spite of her faults. Her courage and love accomplish this happy result and all is well.

140

AT HOME AND ABROAD

Die Glückliche Hand (The Lucky Hand)	Arnold Schonberg (1874-)

American Première: Philadelphia, 1930, with Ivan
Ivantzoff as The Man.
Music drama in one act.

The only singing part is that of The Man. The Woman
and a Handsome Stranger are silent parts. There is a
whispering-speaking chorus of six men and six women,
and in places the chorus is a singing one. The composer
says of the bare story: "A man, laid low by misfortune,
recovers: fortune again smiles on him. He accomplishes
his aims as in earlier days, but nevertheless everything
eventually betrays him. He sinks beneath the renewed
blows of fate.

NOTE: This work was composed in 1913. It was produced in Philadelphia in 1930 by the League of Composers and the Philadelphia
Orchestra, with Stokowski conducting. Schonberg is credited with
the idea of short, condensed opera. *The Lucky Hand* is but 35 minutes long. His *Von Heute auf Morgen* (From One Day to Another)
was produced in Frankfort, Germany, in the season of 1928-29. It
is a comedy opera in which the composer seeks to prove that "his
twelve-tone system can be applied to the expression of light and
cheerful mood."

Orestes	Ernest Krenek (1900-)

Première: Leipsic, 1930.
Legendary opera in five acts.

141

German

Libretto by the composer, who changed the original
   story for dramatic purposes.
Action: Mythological Greece.

   Orestes, son of Agamemnon, disappears from home in
early youth with the aid of his mother, who fears his father
will use him as a sacrifice. Iphegenia is to be sacrificed in
her brother's place but is carried away north to King
Thoas. Agamemnon's wife has a lover who prepares a
poisoned drink and gives it to Electra, who welcomes her
father by giving him the poisoned cup. Electra is murdered. After many years of wandering, Orestes finds Iphegenia and brings her home. The anger of the gods against
Orestes spells doom for him, but their wrath is appeased
and he is allowed peace and rest.

Mr. Wu   D'Albert
                                               (1864-1932)

Première: Dresden, 1932, conducted by Leo Blech,
   intimate friend of the composer, who died before
   his work was finished. The score was completed
   by Blech.
Oriental opera in three acts. Called a "German cousin"
   to play of same name by Harry Vernon and Harold Owen.
Action: China, twentieth century.

   Nang Ping, the innocent young daughter of Wu Ling
Chang, is betrayed by Basil Gregory, son of an English

shipowner. Upon discovering the situation, Wu beheads his daughter and vows revenge. Basil is kidnapped and jailed, Gregory's ships are set on fire, all by Wu's orders. After a time, Mr. Wu invites Mrs. Gregory for a cup of tea while they talk over terms for her son's release. The Chinese servant poisons Wu's tea and thus he is made quickly to join his daughter in their cherry-blossom heaven.

Der Schmied von Gent   Franz Schreker
  (Blacksmith of Ghent)   (1878-1934)

Première: Berlin, 1932.
Fairy opera in three acts and nine scenes.
Book by composer. Story after Chas. de Koster's old
    Flemish tale, *Smetsee Smee.*
Action: Flanders and the Netherlands during the Span-
    ish occupation of the late middle ages.

   Smee is a talkative, light-hearted blacksmith, who has talked too much this time about political matters and has brought evil days upon himself by so doing. He is about to end it all by drowning when three messengers of the devil promise him seven years of plenty in exchange for his soul. Very soon the end of the seven years approaches and he is worried. He does a kindness to the Holy Family and is granted three wishes with which he intends to destroy the evil spirits. But the devil tells him he cannot get around his bargain in that way and takes back his promise to aid. Smee decides to pack up all the provisions he can carry and start out for the heavenly gates. St. Peter will not let him pass, so he takes his provisions and opens a resting place for weary wanderers on the way to those gates. Finally, through a record of good deeds and with the recommendation of the Holy Family, he is let in through the gates and finds peace in the Elysian Fields.

Die Burgschaft	Kurt Weill
(The Pledge)	(1900-)

Première: Berlin, 1932.
Music drama with prologue, three acts and nineteen scenes.
Libretto by Caspar Neher.
Story after fable by Johann Herder. A story of injustice and retribution.
Action: In no-man's land of Urb.

Matthus, a farmer, and Orth, a miller, are friends. Matthus is about to go bankrupt and Orth lends him the needed money, which is to be paid back in installments. This is done. Six years pass and Matthus comes to buy his usual supply of grain from the miller. Orth has only two bags left, but he sells them to his friend. After Matthus leaves, Orth discovers that his son had put all the money they had into one of the bags for safe-keeping. Orth is not anxious for he is sure his friend will return the money. But Matthus does not come back and pretty soon the neighbors are surprised to learn that Matthus has bought a valuable piece of land. Blackmailers pursue him and becoming terrified, he hastens to return the money to Orth. Orth will not take it. It is decided that Matthus' daughter and Orth's son shall marry and the money be given to them, but the daughter runs away from home and bridegroom and goes to the city. Her mother dies of grief. Her father, Matthus, becomes very rich and hard and refuses to give aid to the poor suffering people of the community. He is attacked by a mob and runs to Orth for protection. However, Orth, too, has become hard and turns him over to the mob.

Arabella   Richard Strauss
                                              (1864-1905)

Première: Dresden, 1933.
Lyrical comedy in three acts.
Text by von Hoffmannsthal. Based on his novel,
    Lucidor.
Action: Vienna in the 1860's.

Arabella is the lovely daughter of an aristocratic but very poor family and it is important that she marry a rich husband. Many complications arise through the schemes employed by the family to secure the desired mate. One younger and more beautiful sister, Zdenka, is made to wear boy's clothing lest she prove a competitor in the race. At last the right one arrives, a wealthy land-owner, Mandrika. Just as things are being settled, the younger sister, in love with one of Arabella's other admirers, to gain her point, arouses the jealousy of Mandrika, who thinks her a rival suitor. She finally confesses, Arabella and her wealthy lover are reconciled, and Zdenka and her Austrian Hussar are happy. A double wedding completes the happiness and satisfaction of the family.

145

Michael Kohlhass	Paul von Klenau
	(1883-)

Première: Stuttgart, 1933.
Romantic opera presented in a series of short scenes.
After the novel of the same name by Heinrich von Kleist.

The story is on the theme of the "struggle of the oppressed to obtain justice."

The Favorite	Rudolph Wagner-Regeny
(Der Gunstling)	(1903-)

Première: Dresden, 1935.
Tragic music drama in three acts.
Book by Caspar Neher. After Victor Hugo's drama, *Marie Tudor*, translated into German by George Buchner.
Time: Sixteenth century.

The full title of the opera is *The Favorite*, or *The Last Days of the Great Signor Fabiani*. The story depicts an episode in the career of Mary Tudor, then the consort of Louis XII of France, and her favorite, Fabiani, who arouses her jealousy by his attentions to Jane, the affianced bride and step-daughter of Gil, a workman. Mary causes the execution of her favorite and Jane returns to the arms of her betrothed. The theme seems to be the "good people" against the "evil rulers," according to Neher's story.

AT HOME AND ABROAD

Der Zaubergeige   Verner Egk
(The Magic Fiddle)   (1901-   )

Première: Frankfort-on-Main, 1935.
Première: Berlin, 1936.
Comic folk-opera in three acts.
Text by composer, in collaboration with Ludwig An-
    derson. The plot is a fabulous fairy-tale after a de-
    lightful folk comedy by Pocci.

  Kaspar, a dissatisfied farmhand, with three thalers in his
pocket, sets out to see the world. At the crossroads he
helps a beggar who gives him a violin and tells him that
if he gives up earthly love he will gain riches and fame.
Kaspar becomes a famous violinist and has great riches,
when he is captivated by a beautiful but wicked woman.
Through her wiles he is almost a victim of the gallows,
from which he is saved again by the beggar, who is really
a prince. Kaspar decides that no fame or gold can take
the place of a homelike fireside and the ministrations of
his Gretel.

Die Schweigsame Frau   Richard Strauss
    (Silent Woman)   (1864-1905)

Première: Dresden, 1935. (Did not gain favor) Graz,
    1936. (An unquestionable success.)
Comedy music drama in three acts.
Libretto by Stefen Zweig. Story derived from Ben
    Jonson's delightful farce, *The Silent Woman*. The
    work teems with the newest ideas and fresh in-
    spiration.

147

German

Sir Morosus, an old seaman, cannot stand noise of any kind, and his home is carefully guarded by quiet attendants, his barber and a maid. The sudden visit of a long-lost nephew, Henry, who has married Aminta, leading lady of an opera troupe, upsets the quiet of the household and makes the old uncle furious. He disinherits his nephew on the spot. Henry enters into a plot with his uncle's barber, who promises to find a silent wife for his Lordship. Aminta is chosen and the old uncle falls into the trap. There is a mock marriage, to which come as guests the opera company members, and there is a noisy and hilarious time. The old man is miserable and becomes more so when the "silent wife" turns into a veritable Xantippe. He cries for peace at any price. The plot is revealed, he nobly forgives all, and there is peace and contentment once more in his household.

Andromache	Herbert Windt
	(1892-)

Première: Berlin, 1932.
Legendary music drama.
Composer's libretto freely drawn from story of Racine's tragedy.
Action: Ancient Greece, mythological times.

Andromache, widow of Hector, is loved by Pyrrhus who wishes to marry her. But for political reasons the Grecian princes wish him to marry Hermione, daughter of Menelaus and Helen, although Hermione is already promised to Orestes. She is ambitious, however, and wishes regal power, so she schemes to have Pyrrhus give up his Andromache. He will not, and finally marries Andromache. Hermione, to avenge her wounded pride, persuades Orestes to kill Pyrrhus.

Der Verlorene Sohn	Robert Heger
(Prodigal Son)	(1886-)

Première: Dresden, 1936.
Lyric opera in prologue, two acts, six scenes and epilogue.
Libretto by composer, who borrowed the Biblical story in name only.

A young musician, son of the village organist, is lured away from home by a beautiful woman, an adventuress, who, with her criminal companion, exerts a demon-like power over the boy. His father and young adopted sister never cease hoping and looking for his return. At last, through the continued efforts of the devoted little sister, the prodigal returns home.

Dr. Johannes Faust	Hermann Reutter
	(1900-)

Première: Frankfort, 1936.
Première: Weimar, 1936.
Tragic opera in three acts and five scenes.
Text by Ludwig Anderson. Story after Goethe's *Faust*.

149

The story is the familiar one with a few changes. Faust is first seen in his study when he sells his soul to the devil. The Parma episode is introduced wherein Faust practices his magic art on the Countess who becomes a victim of his power. The opera closes with the devil dragging Faust down into hell.

NOTE: The composer is familiar to the American public as accompanist for Sigrid Onegin. (This is his first opera).

Tartuffe   Hans Haug
                                                    (1900-   )

Première: Basle, 1937.
Comedy opera in two acts.
Libretto by the composer, the five acts of Moliere's play reduced to two.

Under the cloak of religion, Tartuffe becomes the warm friend of a wealthy merchant, Orgon. Tartuffe and the friend's wife, Elmira, fall in love. Orgon, blind to conditions, has unbounded confidence in Tartuffe, who persuades him to deed him his estate. Orgon even offers his daughter Marianne in marriage, although she is already betrothed to Valere. Orgon overhears Tartuffe making love to his wife who reciprocates. Orgon is furious and more so when Tartuffe claims his estate under the deed. However, the King learns of Tartuffe's treachery and deceit and has him thrown into prison.

Massimilla Doni   Othmar Schoeck
(1886-   )

Première: Dresden, 1937.
Lyric drama in four acts and six scenes.
A play within a play. Libretto by Arnim Rueger, after
Balzac's novelette of the same name.
Action: Venice, 1830.

The Duchess Massimilla is in love with the shy and
backward Prince Emilio (Memmi) and snatches him away
from Tinti, the high-strung opera prima donna. The tenor,
Genovese, is so in love with Tinti, his singing partner,
that he forgets his lines in the play. But in the end everything is happily adjusted — the Duchess with her timid
Memmi, and Genovese with his adored Tinti.

Rembrandt van Rijn   Paul von Klenau
(1883-   )

Première: Berlin, 1937.
Tragic opera in four acts. Libretto by the composer,
who, while using the name Rembrandt, has made
a story all his own.
Action: Amsterdam, middle seventeenth century.

Martin Kretzer is a rich man who is ambitious to become a painter, but he has no talent. He consults an alche-
mist to help him gain his desire, but material means fail,
as art cannot be bought. He is advised to get rid of his
powerful competitor, Rembrandt. Then unfolds the tragic
episodes in the life of Rembrandt — bankruptcy, sorrow,
disappointment, domestic tragedies — all tending to warp
his soul, until its final release from the troublous world.

German

Lulu   Alban Berg
                                         (1885-1935)

Première: Zurich, 1937.
Tragic opera in three acts.
Story after Frank Wedekind's plays *Erdgeist* and *Pandora's Box*.
Action: Zurich, Paris, London.

Lulu, tawny-haired wanton, leads many men to ruin. She causes the death of two husbands, ruins the life of a benefactor and becomes mistress to his son. She has a powerful, demonlike influence over every one coming in her way. She is imprisoned for murder but breaks out. She finally meets her death in a wretched London garret, being killed by her last lover, a veritable Jack-the-Ripper. Her loyal friend, Countess Geschwitz, who stands by her to the last, is killed by the same hand.

NOTE: This was a posthumous work. Dr. Willy Reich, the Austrian critic, says in Musical America of July, 1937: "The première might be considered a musical world sensation; Berg's friends had gathered from far and near, likewise representatives of the world press . . . . Definite musical forms are associated with the individual characters, which forms run through the whole piece."

GERMAN OPERA

(PART II)

composed before 1900

and presented *for the first time*

in the United States during the

*XX*TH *Century*

(in prominent Opera Houses), also

Outstanding Revivals in the United States

during the same period

1900 — Season 1937–1938

(inclusive)

German

Die Zauberflote	Mozart
(Magic Flute)	(1756-1791)

Première: Vienna, 1791.
Première: New York, 1833. American Première. Park
    Theatre, in an English adaptation.
Première: First time at Metropolitan Opera House,
      1900, in Italian, with Marcella Sembrich as the
      Queen of Night, Emma Eames as Pamina, Andre-
      as Dippel as Tamino, Giuseppe Campanari as
      Papageno, Pol Plancon as Sarastro.
Symbolic opera in two acts.
Libretto by Schikander and Gieske from the story
    Lulu, or the Magic Flute, by Wieland.
Action: Egypt, time of Rameses I.

Sarastro the High Priest has taken Pamina away from
the bad influence of her mother, the Queen of Night. Her
mother is seeking and secures the aid of Tamino, whose
life has been saved from a terrible serpent by three of
the Queen's young women attendants. The Queen gives
Tamino a magic flute and the companionship of a fantastic
character, the bird catcher, Papageno, on the journey.
They find Pamina and the young people fall in love. Sarastro promises them a happy future provided they endure
many difficulties and overcome them successfully. They
pass through all the tests with great courage and are finally
united, in spite of the interference of the wicked Queen
and much to her vexation. So that all ends quite happily
for the young lovers.

Parsifal Richard Wagner
(1813-1883)

Première: Bayreuth, 1882.

Première: New York, Metropolitan Opera House, 1903, American Première, with Alois Burgstaller as Parsifal, Milka Ternina as Kundry, Otto Goritz (American debut) as Klingsor, Anton van Rooy as Amfortas, Marcel Journet as Titurel, Robert Blass as Gurnemanz, Louise Homer as the Mystic Voice.

Festival drama in three acts.

Text by composer, based on the famous *Legend of the Grail*.

Action: Spain at Monsalvat, near and in the Castle of the Holy Grail; Klingsor's enchanted garden and castle, in the Middle Ages.

Amfortas, King of the Knights of the Holy Grail, is enticed into the garden of Klingsor, by Kundry. While in her embrace, he drops the holy spear and Klingsor seizes it, wounds Amfortas and takes it away with him. The wound can be healed only by a touch of the spear, which can be regained only by one who is sinless. Parsifal proves such an one. He regains the spear, destroys Klingsor, whose death frees Kundry from his wicked spell, heals the wound of Amfortas by a touch of the spear, and becomes King of the Knights.

NOTE: The performance at the Metropolitan Opera House in 1903 was the first outside of Bayreuth, overruling the legal protest of Wagner's widow.

Allegorically, the play brings out the triumph of Christianity over Paganism, Parsifal representing Christianity and Klingsor Paganism.

German

Hansel and Gretel   Humperdinck
                                       (1854-1921)
Première: Munich, 1893.
Première: New York, Daly's Theatre, 1895.
Première: New York, Metropolitan Opera House,
      1905, with Lina Abarbanell as Hansel, Bella Alten
      as Gretel, Otto Goritz as the Father, Marion Weed
      as the Mother, Louise Homer as the Witch.
Fairy opera with prelude and three acts.
Story after the Grimm's fairy tale, *Babes in the Wood.*
Text by Wette.

   Hansel and Gretel are sent into the woods to gather
strawberries. It becomes dark and they lose their way.
They go to sleep and on waking see the Witch's ginger-
bread hut and being hungry they begin to nibble on it.
The wicked old Witch seizes Hansel and puts him into a
pen to fatten him and she makes Gretel help her. The
oven is red hot. The Witch mumbles her magic spell and
Gretel hears it. The Witch takes Hansel out of the pen.
While she stands in front of the oven the children repeat
the spell, push her in and shut the door. There is a great
crash. The oven has fallen apart and all the fence ginger-
bread children come to life. Father, Mother and all sing a
hymn of praise to God.

The Taming of the Shrew   Hermann Goetz
                                       (1840-1876)
Première: Mannheim, 1874.
Première: New York, National Opera Company,
      1886.

Première: New York, Metropolitan Opera House, 1916, with Marguerite Ober as Katherine, Clarence Whitehill as Petruchio, Marie Rappold as Bianca.
Comic opera in four acts.
Text by Widmann. Story after Shakespeare.
Action: Italy; Padua and vicinity, Middle Ages.

Baptista, a nobleman of Padua, has two daughters, Katherine and Bianca. Katherine is a veritable shrew and her gentle sister cannot marry until she is out of the way. Petruchio, a gentleman of Verona, has the courage to woo Katherine in spite of her hateful temper. On their wedding day he begins to tame her and finally succeeds in making her a most exemplary and obedient wife, wholly subservient to his wishes.

Saint Elizabeth
(Miracle of Roses)

Franz Liszt
(1811-1886)

Première: Weimar, 1881. First performance as an opera.
Première: New York, Metropolitan Opera House, 1918, (United States Première) with Florence Easton as Elizabeth, Clarence Whitehill as the Landgrave Ludwig.
Lyric drama with prologue and three acts. First written as an oratorio.
Action: Thuringia, time of the Crusades.

German

Elizabeth, beloved wife of the Landgrave Ludwig, secretly takes food and clothing to the poor, directly against his orders. One day he meets her in the forest and asks what is in her well-filled scarf. She answers, "Roses." By a miracle the food had been changed to roses! She confesses the truth to her husband and together they thank God for this blessing. He becomes a Crusader and falls in battle. Sophie, his mother, ambitious to be ruler in his stead, turns the widow and her children out of the castle. They are cared for by the poor whom she has befriended. She continues to minister to their wants until death finally comes to her.

Oberon	von Weber
(Elf-king's Oath)	(1786-1826)

Première: London, 1826. Conducted by the composer, who was in ill health at the time and passed away two months later.

Première: New York, 1828, Park Theatre.

Première: First time at the Metropolitan Opera House, 1918, in English, with Rosa Ponselle as Rezia, Martinelli as Sir Huon, Althouse as Oberon, Alice Gentle as Fatima.

Fairy romantic opera in three acts.

Text by Planche.

Action: Imaginary land of elves and fairies.

Oberon, King of the Fairies, quarrels with his wife, Titania, and declares he will have nothing more to do with her until he can find a maid and a man who can stand any test of their love. Huon and Rezia, the Caliph's daughter, he thinks are the pair. He gives Huon a magic horn to use to ward off danger. Rezia, in the harem of Emir, trembles at the thought of marrying the Persian Prince, Babekan. Huon comes to the wedding feast. A blast from the horn and all fall asleep. He kills the Prince and flees with Rezia to the garden of Oberon, where they are found by Emir and are about to be burned when a blast from the horn frightens the Moslems, who disperse. Oberon and Titania appear and escort the happy pair to the court of Charlemagne. Oberon and Titania are reunited and all ends happily.

The Elopement from the Seraglio (sometimes called *The Abduction*)	Mozart (1756-1791)

Première: Vienna, 1782.

Première: New York, 1862, in German at the old German Opera House.

Première: New York, 1927, in English by the Rochester (afterwards American) Opera Company, with Ethel Codd as Constanza, Albert Newcomb as Belmonte, George Fleming Houston as Osmin, Charles Hadley as Pedrillo.

Oriental comedy opera in three acts.

Action: A country house of Bassa, sixteenth century.

The beautiful Christian girl, Constance, has been sold to the Turkish Pasha Selim by the pirates who kidnapped her. She is imprisoned in the harem of Selim, where Belmonte, her lover, learning her whereabouts, gains entrance by strategy. They plan escape, and with the friendly aid of Pedrillo, the Pasha's gardener, they have almost succeeded when they are caught by Oemin, the overseer of the seraglio. The Pasha at first threatens to have them both killed, but being kind-hearted, he allows them to go free.

Der Freischütz
(The Freeshooter)

von Weber
(1786-1826)

Première: Berlin, 1821.
Première: New York, Park Theatre, 1825.
Première: New York, Metropolitan Opera House, 1924, important revival, with Elizabeth Rethberg as Agatha, Curt Taucher as Max, Michael Bohnen as Cuno, Gustave Schutzendorf as Prince Ottokar.
Romantic opera in three acts.
Text by Friedrick Kind (re-arranged several times by other writers). Story founded on an old German tradition.
Action: Bohemia, shortly after the Seven Years' War.

Max and Caspar, assistant huntsmen to Cuno, head ranger on the estate of Prince Ottokar, are about to enter a contest in sharp-shooting, to be witnessed by the Prince. Caspar is ambitious to win so that he may obtain higher service in the Prince's employ. Max, to whom Cuno has promised his daughter in marriage if he wins the contest, is discouraged because he has not been doing very well in practice. Caspar, ambitious and sly, has sold himself to the devil for seven magic bullets, six sure shots are for him, the seventh for the devil to use as he wishes. He tells Caspar to bring another buyer for more bullets when his six are gone or it will be bad luck to him. Caspar persuades Max to be the buyer. Agatha begs Max to keep away from the Devil's Glen but he will not listen and secures the bullets. Agatha prays for his safety. In the end, Caspar is wounded and carried off by the devil, a rich young peasant wins the contest and poor Max and Agatha are disconsolate. However, Max is forgiven, happy days return, and they are wedded.

| *Tristan and Isolde* | Richard Wagner |
| | (1813-1883) |

Première: Munich, 1865.

Première: New York, 1886, Metropolitan Opera House.

Outstanding recent revival, 1935, February, Metropolitan Opera House, with Kirsten Flagstad * as Isolde, Lauritz Melchior as Tristan, Maria Olszewska as Brangane, Ludwig Hoffmann as King Mark, Friedrich Schorr as Kurwenal, Hans Clemens as Melot.

Tragic music drama in three acts.

Book by the composer. Story after ancient Celtic legend.

Action: Cornwall, Brittany, ancient times.

* Her initial appearance at the Metropolitan in this role. Mme. Flagstad's Isolde is now acknowledged as "the incomparable one of this era."

German

King Mark of Cornwall sends his nephew, Tristan, to bring to him Isolde, daughter of the King of Ireland, to be his Queen. Tristan (before the story opens) had slain Isolde's betrothed. He was badly wounded, but Isolde nursed him back to health meaning to kill him with the very sword which had taken the life of her beloved. Instead, she falls in love with him. On the ship she orders her maid, Brangane, to prepare poison for the wine to be served them, but instead, Brangane prepares a love potion, which they both drink, and there is an ardent love scene. After they land at Cornwall King Mark learns of his treachery, and Tristan is fatally wounded by Melot, one of the King's knights. Tristan is taken to his home in Brittany by his faithful henchman, Kurwenal, and Isolde follows, arriving just in time to see him expire. She breathes her last over his dead body.

The Flying Dutchman   Richard Wagner
(Der Fliegende Hollander)   (1813-1883)

Première: Dresden, 1843.
Première: New York, 1877, Academy of Music.
Première: First time Metropolitan Opera House, 1889.
        Recent outstanding revival at the Metropolitan Opera House, 1937, January, with Kirsten Flagstad as Senta (Research reveals her as the first native-born Norwegian to sing the part at the Metropolitan), Kerstin Thorborg as Mary, Charles Kullman as Eric, Friedrich Schorr as the Dutchman, Emanuel List as Daland.
Music drama in three acts. Book by the composer.

162

AT HOME AND ABROAD

Story based on Heine's version of an old legend.
Action: Norwegian fishing village, eighteenth century.

The Dutchman, Vanderdecken, having sworn to double the Cape of Good Hope in spite of a terrific storm, if it should take all eternity to do so, is condemned by the devil to sail the seas until a woman, by her undying love, shall redeem him from the curse. He is permitted to land once in seven years to search for her. Senta, lovely daughter of Daland, a Norwegian sea captain, is fascinated by the story of the Dutchman and daily gazes at the picture of him which hangs in her home. Her heart is filled with pity for him and she dreams that perhaps she may be the maid who will free him. Eric, her village lover, tries to persuade her to forget her foolish idea and marry him but she will not listen. Daland returns from a voyage and with him comes a stranger. It is the Dutchman, and he and Senta gaze long into each other's eyes. In time their betrothal follows. Eric upbraids her and the Dutchman overhears. Concluding that she will in the same fashion, prove unfaithful to him, he rushes to his ship, which immediately leaves the shore. Senta follows. Calling after him that she is "faithful unto death," she throws herself from the cliff into the sea. The curse is lifted and they float heavenward as the phantom ship disappears.

Falstaff   Verdi
                                              (1813-1901)

Première: Milan, 1893. (The composer's last opera.)
Première: First time in New York, 1895.
          Notable revival, Metropolitan Opera House,

163

1925, when the now great American baritone, Lawrence Tibbett, created a sensation in his characterization of Ford, and became famous overnight in the operatic world. The principal characters in that production were: Lucrezia Bori as Mistress Ford, Antonio Scotti as Falstaff, Lawrence Tibbett as Ford, Beniamino Gigli as Fenton.

Comic opera in three acts.

Libretto by Boito, based on Shakespeare's *Henry IV*, and *Merry Wives of Windsor*.

Action: England. Reign of Henry IV.

Sir John Falstaff, full of conceit, believes that no woman can resist his charms. He writes love letters to Mistress Ford and Mistress Page, worded identically the same. The ladies compare notes and plan to make a fool of him. An appointment is made for Falstaff to come to the Ford home. While there, a commotion is heard in the hall. Ford, young Fenton (in love with Anne Ford), and Dr. Caius (also in love with Anne), have come to find the offender. Falstaff is hastily concealed and is finally pushed into a laundry basket. Mrs. Ford orders the servants to throw the basket out of the window. As her husband enters, she takes him to the window and points downward. All laugh heartily. A second prank is planned—a midnight rendezvous in the forest. Falstaff finds himself surrounded by masked imps, witches, fairies, who knock and jeer him. Finally discovering that it is the Ford household and friends that are the culprits he confesses that he has made an ass of himself and invites them all to a midnight feast. Ford is persuaded to bless the union of Anne and Fenton, to the chagrin of Dr. Caius, and all ends merrily.

RUSSIAN OPERA

(PART I)

composed and produced abroad,

in the United States, or in both,

during the

*XX*TH *Century*

1900 — Season 1937–1938

(inclusive)

Character of Russian Opera

Glinka originated Russian National Opera. In his first opera, *A Life for the Czar*, Russian folk tunes prevail. He introduced Oriental coloring later, and this is evident in opera of other Russian composers. The American Encyclopedia of Music says, "As the founder of an original Russian School he stands among the epoch-makers in music."

The Slavonic race is divided into tribes. Russia is here treated under its own head, because it has evolved a distinct and national musical art.

St. Petersburg was changed to Petrograd in 1914. It became Leningrad in 1924.

165

Russian

The Invisible City of Kitezh Rimsky-Korsakov
(1844-1908)

Première: St. Petersburg, 1907.

Première: Philadelphia, 1936, (American Première), by the Art of Musical Russia, Inc., and the Philadelphia Orchestra, with Jeanne Palmer as Fevronia, Ivan Velikanoff as the Prince.

Première: New York, Metropolitan Opera House, with same company, the next month, 1936.

Legendary opera in four acts and six scenes.

Text by Bielsky, narrative based on *The Chronicles of Kitezh*, a cycle of legends.

Action: Near Novgorod, Russia.

A strange youth finds Fevronia in the forest and falls in love with her. He proves to be the Prince Vsevolod of Kitezh. The destruction of the city is predicted. As Fevronia's bridal procession passes, she is dragged off by the Tartars. She prays that the city may be made invisible. The Prince, angry at Fevronia's capture, goes out and is killed. Fevronia is bound to a cart in the camp of the Tartars. She escapes while they sleep. In the morning the city has disappeared. Fevronia's prayer has been answered. The city has been moved to God's heaven and here she greets her Prince, who tells her that he was slain but is now alive, and both know that life is everlasting.

Le Coq D'Or Rimsky-Korsakov
(The Golden Cockerel) (1844-1908)

Première: Moscow, 1910.

Première: New York, (American Première), Metro-

politan Opera House, 1918, Michael Fokine's stage version was used, calling for a double cast. Marie Barrientos (singer), Rosina Galli (dancer) as the Queen, Adamo Didur (singer) Adolf Bohm (dancer), as the King, Rafaelo Diaz (singer), Bonfiglio (dancer), as the Astrologer.
Tragi-comedy opera in three acts. Book by Bielsky.
Story founded on the poem of Pushkin.
Action: Russia, early nineteenth century.

The Astrologer presents King Dodon with a Cock of Gold, which will always cry if there is danger. The Cock cries and the King's sons go out with their army. They do not return and are found by King Dodon dead on the battlefield. The King sees Queen Shemaka coming out of her tent and is fascinated with her. She consents to become his bride. When they return to Dodon's royal city, the Astrologer appears and claims the Queen as payment for the Cock. Dodon kills him. The Golden Cock picks out Dodon's brains; a thunderstorm and darkness comes; the Cock and the Queen disappear, she laughing, while the people mourn for their silly King.

NOTE: The opera was finished in 1907, but performance was forbidden until three years later, owing to political censure. It was believed that King Dodon was a musical portrait of the then Czar Nicholas.

The Fair at Sorotshinsk   Moussorgsky
                                             (1835-1881)
Première: Moscow, 1913.
Première: New York, Metropolitan Opera House,
        1930, with Maria Müller as Parassia, Frederick

Jagel as Gritzko, Ezio Pinza as Tcherevick, the father, Ina Bourskaya as Khivria the step-mother, George Cehanovsky as the Gypsy.
Comic opera in three acts.
Story by the composer after Gogol's stories of Ukrainian life.
Action: A village in Little Russia.

At the Fair, Parassia, daughter of the farmer Tcherevick, meets the handsome young Gritzko and the young people fall in love. The father is satisfied but Gritzko knows that the step-mother will not be. So he secures the aid of a Gypsy. Tcherevick, berated and abused by his wife upon his return home, calls in his friends and they begin drinking and carousing. During the festivities there is a great noise at the door, a window flies open, the door opens of its own accord and the superstitious company begins to tell frightening tales. The Gypsy appears with some of the young people of the village. The drunken guests cry out that the devil is loose and there is great confusion. The step-mother's lover is revealed in his hiding-place and Tcherevick, now master of the situation, consents to the celebration of the wedding of Gritzko and Parassia.

NOTE: This was a posthumous opera edited by three different persons, but the version used at the Metropolitan is the one of Nicholas Tcherepnin.

Le Rossignol   Igor Stravinsky
(The Nightingale)   (1882-   )
Première: Paris, 1914.
Première: New York, Metropolitan Opera House,

1926, with Marion Talley as the Nightingale and Adamo Didur as the Emperor of China.

Fairy opera in three episodes.

Text by composer and Mitousoff, after fairy tale of Hans Christian Andersen.

The Emperor is greatly depressed. His officials bring him a little bird whose song so pleases him that he is quite restored to his good humor. Presently the Japanese envoys bring in a gorgeous mechanical bird and the little nightingale disappears. This so distresses the Emperor that he becomes very ill. The little bird returns and sings away his pain—sings all night, chasing away death. When the courtiers arrive next morning expecting to find their Emperor dead, instead he greets them with a happy "Good morning!"

Love of Three Oranges   Serge Prokofieff
(1891-   )

Première: Chicago, 1921, (World Première), with Jose Mojica as the Prince, Nina Koshetz as the Witch, Fata Morgana, Jeanne Dusseau as Ninette. Conducted by composer.

Première: New York, Manhattan Opera House, 1922, with Chicago company.

Fantastic opera with prologue, four acts and ten scenes.

Text by composer after fairy tale by Gozzi. The work is ultra-modern and has been called "the most amusing burlesque of the day."

The Prince has been poisoned and is very ill. A hearty laugh will cure him. An ugly witch, cast out of the palace,

169

turns a somersault at which the Prince laughs and is cured. But the witch calls down a curse on him and tells him that he must love three oranges and will not be happy until his love is returned. He finds the three oranges. In each is an enchanted Princess. When released two of them die of thirst, but the third, Ninette, is saved by being given water at once. After some mysterious happenings all ends well and the lovers live happily ever after.

Mavra   Stravinsky
                                                 (1882-   )

Première: Paris, 1922.

Première: Philadephia, 1935, (United States Première) with all Russian cast — Maria Kurenko as Parasha, the daughter, Ivan Ivantzoff as the Hussar, Lydia Koretsky as the Neighbor, Nadina Fedora as the Mother.

Comic opera in one act.

Text by Boris Kochno, story after a tale by Pushkin.

Action: St. Petersburg. 1840.

A new maid is needed in the house. The daughter thinks she has found a way to see more often her Hussar lover and persuades him to don woman's clothes and apply for the job. Her mother engages the new "maid" and all goes well until one day the Mother returns unexpectedly with a neighbor, to find the new maid shaving ! !

NOTE: The opera is but 24 minutes long and is a parody on old Italian opera.

AT HOME AND ABROAD
Russian

Lady Macbeth of Mzensk	Dmitri Shostakovitch (1906-)

Première: Leningrad, 1934.
Première: Cleveland, 1935, (American Première) by the Art of Musical Russia, Inc., with Anna Leskaya as Katrina, Elena Shrvedova as Sonetka, Ivan Ivantzoff as Sergei, Ivan Velikanoff as Zinova, Rodzinski conducted, with the Cleveland Orchestra.
Première: New York première, Metropolitan Opera House three days later with same company.
Tragic opera in four acts and nine scenes.
Libretto by composer with A. Preis from story by Nikolai Leskoff.
Action: Russia, 1840.

Katrina is the wife of the rich Russian merchant, Zinova. Boris, her father-in-law nags her continually. She is wretchedly unhappy, lonely, childless, and her life is one of idleness. The new clerk, Sergei, is a sly hypocrite who works on her loneliness to gain her love. She becomes distracted with the nagging of Boris and poisons him. After a long absence Zinova returns and discovers conditions between his wife and Sergei, and when he quarrels with Katrina he is killed by Sergei, who can now become Katrina's lawful husband. They have dragged Zinova's body to the cellar. When the marriage is about to take place, the body is discovered by some drunken peasants who come to steal. This news is brought to the police by a sergeant who also tells of the marriage which is to take place. The police scent graft. The pair are exposed by the greedy-for-spoils sergeant and they are sent to Siberia. On the way, Sergei transfers his affections to Sonetka, a fellow prisoner and makes a fool of Katrina who, mad with jealousy, pushes Sonetka, into the water and then drowns herself as well.

NOTE: This is the first Soviet opera to reach the United States. The first European première outside Russia took place at Bratislava, 1936.

RUSSIAN OPERA

(PART II)

composed *before 1900*

and presented *for the first time*

in the United States during the

*XX*TH *Century*

(in prominent Opera Houses), also

outstanding revivals in the United

States during the same period

1900 — Season 1937–1938

(inclusive)

Russian

Pique Dame	Tschaikowsky
(Queen of Spades)	(1840-1893)

Première: St. Petersburg, 1890.

Première: New York, (American Première) Metropolitan Opera House, 1910, with Emmy Destinn as Lisa, Anna Meitschik as the Countess, the Queen of Spades, Leo Slezak as Herman.

Tragic opera in three acts.

Libretto by Modeste Tschaikowsky, brother of the composer, after a prose tale of Pushkin.

Action: St. Petersburg, end of eighteenth century.

Herman, a poor Hussar, is in love with Lisa, who, however, is engaged to a rich Prince. Herman hopes to win enough gold to obtain her. He is a gambler. Lisa's grandmother, the Queen of Spades has a secret to a three-card combination that always wins. Lisa tells Herman how to get it, but the grandmother dies of fright when he enters her room. He is haunted by the dead woman's voice which repeats the combination. Lisa begs·him not to use it but he insists, and she drowns herself. He goes to the gaminghouse and wins twice. The third time he stakes all he has won. The wrong card turns up—the Queen of Spades! The spectre face of the old grandmother looks at him across the table. He is terrified and stabs himself.

Boris Goudonov	Moussorgsky
	(1835-1881)

Première: St. Petersburg, 1874.

Première: New York, Metropolitan Opera House,

1913, with Adamo Didur as Boris, Leonora Sparks
as Xenia, Louise Homer as Mariana, Paul Althouse
as Dimitri. Toscanini conducted.
Tragic opera in three acts.
Book by the composer, based on drama by Pushkin.
Action: Russia, about 1600.

Dimitri, son of the Czar, and rightful heir to the throne,
has been murdered secretly by Boris Goudonov who is
crowned instead. A young novice, Gregory, determined
to punish Boris, pretends to be Dimitri. Mariana, a Polish
lady is in love with him and is ambitious, so she urges him
to claim the throne. When Boris hears that the Poles have
received the false Dimitri, there is a terrible scene of remorse and despair. Dimitri is marching to Moscow at the
head of his soldiers. A council is held in the Kremlin to
decide the fate of Dimitri. Boris presides. He is consumed
with fear and goes mad and dies in terror, declaring his
young son as his successor.

NOTE: The part of Boris is one of the outstanding roles of the great
Russian, Feodor Chaliapin, who sang it first at the Metropolitan
in 1921.

Prince Igor   Borodin
                                    (1834-1887)
Première: St. Petersburg, 1890.
Première: New York, Metropolitan Opera House,
        1916, with Frances Alda as Jaroslavna, Pasquale
        Amato as Prince Igor, Luca Botta as Vladimir,
        Adamo Didur as Prince Galitsky and also as the
        Tartar Khan.

Russian

Romantic opera with prologue and four acts. Text by
the composer and Stassoff.
Story based on an old historical Russian chronicle.
Action: Russia, twelfth century.

Prince Igor and his son Vladimir go out to battle against
the Tartars. Jaroslavna, his wife, is left in charge of Prince
Galitsky, brother of Igor, who is also to look after the
affairs of the government during Igor's absence. Prince
Igor and his son are captured by the Tartars. Vladimir
falls in love with the daughter of the Tartar Khan. Prince
Igor escapes but Vladimir is held by the girl and they are
wed with the approval of the old Khan. Igor returns home
to find that his brother has seized the power and caused
unhappiness to Jaroslavna. Amidst the ringing of bells the
Princess and the people welcome Prince Igor with thanks-
giving.

NOTE: This is Borodin's only opera. He died before its completion
and Rimsky-Korsakov and Glazounoff finished it.

Eugen Onegin   Tschaikowsky
                                              (1840-1893)
Première: Moscow, 1879.
Première: New York, Metropolitan Opera House,
          1920, with Claudia Muzio as Titania, Martinelli
          as Lenski, de Luca as Onegin, Adamo Didur as
          Prince Gremin.
Lyric tragedy in three acts. Text by composer and
          Shilovsky.
Story based on Pushkin's romance.

Action: An estate near St. Petersburg.
   In St. Petersburg, second decade of nineteenth century.

Eugen Onegin, a Don Juan, inherits an estate and comes to take possession. His friend, Lenski, introduces him to a family of landed gentry in which are two charming daughters, Olga and Titania. Olga is engaged to Lenski. Titania is a romantic young girl who comes to idealize Eugen. Feeling however his unfitness for domestic life, he discourages her, but to amuse himself he begins a flirtation with Olga. This leads to disaster—a duel with his friend, whom he kills. Years after, Eugen attends a reception given by the Princess Gremina in St. Petersburg, and discovers her to be Titania. He tries to make love to her but is repulsed. So the wretched man leaves and pursues his aimless wandering through the world.

The Czar's Bride	Rimsky-Korsakov (1844-1908)

Première: Moscow, 1896. Privately produced.
Première: New York, first performance, 1922, Amsterdam Theatre, by the Art of Musical Russia, Inc., with Zenia Ershova (borrowed from *Chauve Souris*) as Lubasha.
Première: New York, Lewisohn Stadium, 1936, with Maria Kurenko as Martha, Ivan Velikanoff as Lykov, Edwina Eustis as Lubasha, George Dubrowsky as Gryaznoy, Michail Shvetz as Sobakin.
Tragic opera in four acts.

Russian

Libretto by Tyumenev, story after a drama by Mey.
Action: Novgorod, Russia, in the days of Ivan the
Terrible, sixteenth century.

Gryaznoy, a guardsman, is madly in love with Martha,
daughter of the rich Sobakin. Martha is engaged to Lykov.
Gryaznoy's mistress, Lubasha, overhears him ask the court
physician for a love potion with which to win the love
of Martha. Czar Ivan sees Martha and is infatuated with
her beauty. Martha, her father, Gryaznoy, and Lykov
are at table when a message comes from the Czar to tell
Martha that she is to be his wife. Gryaznoy has just
dropped the love potion into Martha's cup. Later, Martha,
now the bride of the Czar, lies ill in the Kremlin. When
she is told that Lykov has been executed by the Czar
through jealousy of her love, she goes mad. Lubasha confesses that she had substituted a slow poison for the love
potion which Martha had drunk. Gryaznoy kills her and
is himself executed.

NOTE: The Art of Musical Russia is a company of Russian refugees.

Snegourotchka	Rimsky-Korsakov
(The Snow Maiden)	(1844-1908)

Première: St. Petersburg, 1882.
Première: New York, Metropolitan Opera House,
    1922, with Lucrezia Bori as Snegourotchka, Mario
    Laurenti as Mizguir, Raymonde Delaunois as
    Lehl, Orville Harrold as the Czar, Yvonne d'Arle
    as Kupava, Leon Rothier as King Winter, father
    of the Snow-Maiden.

178

AT HOME AND ABROAD
Russian

Fairy opera with prologue and four acts.
Text by Ostrovesky. Story based on Russian folk-lore.
Action: Imaginary province of Berendey, ruled over
by a benevolent old Czar. Prehistoric days of old
Russia.

The young Tartar, Mizguir, falls in love with the Snow-
Maiden while she is visiting among mortals. She loves the
shepherd Lehl. Mizguir's abandoned love, Kopava, com-
plains to the Czar that the Snow-Maiden has wronged
her, but the beauty of the Snow-Maiden saves her from
harm. She begs her mother to let her love as mortals do
and her wish is granted. But when Mizguir claims her, a
ray of sunlight melts her completely and Mizguir kills
himself.

Khovanchina   Moussorgsky
                                                       (1835-1881)

Amateur Production: St. Petersburg, 1886.
Privately presented: St. Petersburg, 1898, by Mamon-
toff's Private Opera Company.
Première: (First public performance)
St. Petersburg, 1911, with Chaliapin as Dositheus.
Première: New York (first time) by the Russkaya
Grand Opera Company (Russians) in Mecca
Auditorium, March, 1931, with Max Pantelieff as
Dositheus, Michail Shvetz as Ivan Khovansky,
A. Alexandroff as Galitsin, Alex Kourganoff as
Andrew, Valia Valentinova as Martha.

179

Tragic folk-opera in five acts.
Story based on historic events in Russia.
Action: Russia during the reign of Peter the Great.

In Russia during the time of the story, several sects were distinct, and continual friction was the result. Prince Khovansky of the Conservative element of the Old Believers urges his followers to resist even to the death the modern ideas of the Czar. Dositheus, religious leader of the Old Believers, saves Martha, a discarded mistress of Ivan's dissolute son, Andrew. Ivan and Dositheus try to convince Prince Galitsin of the Culturals that only religion can make Russia safe. Continual resistance to the new ideas results in tragedy for the sects. Ivan is murdered. Galitsin is led away into exile. Martha finally wins back Andrew and he embraces her faith and joins the Old Believers, when, rather than submit to capture by foreign mercenaries, they build a pyre which they ascend amid continual chanting. There is a great ringing of bells and the blast of trumpets as they perish in the flames.

NOTE: This was a posthumous opera, completed and orchestrated by Rimsky-Korsakov.

Sadko   Rimsky-Korsakov
                                              (1844-1908)
Première: Moscow, 1898.
Première: New York, Metropolitan Opera House,
        1930 (American Première) with Edward Johnson
        as Sadko, Ina Bourskaya as his young wife, Edith
        Fleischer as Volkhova, Pavel Ludikar as the King

of the Sea, George Cehanovsky as the Apparition. Lyric legend in three acts and seven scenes. Text by the composer aided by Bielsky.
Story taken from several versions of the Epic of Sadko.
Action: Novgorod, eleventh century. An ancient Russian myth.

Sadko, a minstrel of Novgorod, wanders to the moonlit shore of the lake and pours out his soul in song. He sees the swans on the lake transformed into the Sea Princess, Volkhova, and her attendants. His music has won her love and they pledge their troth. As she leaves, she tells him if he will cast his net into the lake he will draw out three goldfish. He does so, and they turn to gold bullion. He buys a fleet of ships and sails into foreign lands in search of wealth. At the end of a number of years he has become rich. The Sea King is angry that Sadko has not paid him tribute and summons him to his Ocean Palace. Sadko here finds the Princess, and the King, charmed with Sadko's music, gives his daughter to him in marriage. He instructs Sadko to play his wildest music in celebration and all the inhabitants of the sea break into a mad frenzy of dancing. Suddenly a ghost appears, strikes Sadko's harp from his hands and orders him to return to Novgorod. Sadko and the Princess return to earth. The Princess makes him a bed of rushes and sings him to sleep. She weeps over him and is transformed into the river Volkhova. Sadko is awakened by the voice of his wife whom he has so neglected. He promises never to leave her again. Together they watch the flowing river Volkhova which has opened the way from Novgorod to the sea. He thinks he has been dreaming, when, lo! his ships come sailing up the river!

Russian

A Life for the Czar	Glinka
	(1804-1857)

Première: St. Petersburg, 1836.

Première: New York, February, 1936, excerpts from the opera by the Schola Cantorum, conducted by Hugh Ross.

Première: American Première, in its entirety as an opera, San Francisco, December, 1936, in celebration of the centennial of its first production — in the Tivoli Opera House by the Russian Music Society of San Francisco, with Yasha Davidoff specially imported for the role of Ivan.

Tragic opera in four acts and epilogue.

Action: Russia, 1633—time of the Russian-Polish War.

Ivan Soussanin, a Russian patriot, is celebrating the marriage of his daughter Antonida with her soldier lover, Sobinin, just back from the wars. A messenger rushes in to say that the Russians are in retreat. Soon Polish soldiers burst into Ivan's hut and demand that he lead them to the young Czar Michael Romanov. Ivan whispers to his young son, Vanya, to warn the Czar, and then pretends to obey the command of the Poles. But he leads them in another direction. When this is discovered, the Poles kill Ivan. The Czar safely escapes. Thus Ivan gives a life for the czar.

NOTE: Other singers of the San Francisco cast included Sophia Samorukova, Gabriel Leonoff, Tatiana Popova, Nicolas Molotoff, all members of the local Russian colony. Paul Shulgin conducted.

SLAVIC OPERA

(PART I)

composed and produced abroad, in
the United States, or in both,
during the
*XX*TH *Century*
1900 — Season 1937–1938
(inclusive)

Placed under this general title are
*POLISH, CZECK, BULGARIAN,
CROATIAN, BOHEMIAN*

Bedrick Smetana was the founder of the
Bohemian Nationalist School of Opera.

NOTE: In 1918, the Czeckoslovakian Republic was established from the territories of the former Austro-Hungar-
ian monarchy, including Bohemia, Moravia and other
minorities.

Slavic

Manru   Paderewski
                                                (1860-   )

Première: Dresden, 1901.
Première: New York, Metropolitan Opera House,
    1902, with Sembrich as Ulana, Alex van Bandrow-
    ski as Manru, Fritzi Scheff as Asa, Adolph Muhl-
    mann as Oros.
Tragic opera in three acts.
Story after a Polish romance by Nossig.
Action: Hungary, early nineteenth century.
  Ulana, a village girl, marries the gypsy, Manru. He
leaves home because he cannot stand the crying of their
baby. He steals the affections of Asa, the beloved of Oros.
Poor Ulana drowns herself. Oros pushes Manru into the
same lake in which Ulana's body lies, and he drowns.

Jenufa   Leos Janacek
                                               (1854-1928)

Première: Prague, 1916.
Première: New York, Metropolitan Opera House,
    1924, with Marie Jeritza as Jenufa, Rudolf Laub-
    enthal as Stewa, Merlin Ohman as Laca, Margaret
    Matzenauer as the Foster-Mother.
Tragic opera in three acts.
Text after a play by Gabriele Preiss. A tale of Moravian
    peasant life.
Action: Among the hills of Moravia.

184

Stewa has betrayed Jenufa, adopted daughter of a devoted foster-mother. Jenufa loves Stewa and avoids Laca, his step-brother, who loves her. Laca, angry with Jenufa because she will not notice her, slashes her across the cheek and spoils her beauty. When Jenufa's child is born, the foster-mother tells Stewa of it but he rushes out saying he will not wed Jenufa as he is to marry another. The mother, thinking to bring about Jenufa's marriage with Laca, who is good and steady, gives Jenufa a sleeping potion, takes the child to the frozen river and pushes it under the ice, telling Jenufa that it has died. Laca still wishes to marry Jenufa in spite of the child and the wedding preparations are being made when the corpse of the child is found, the mother confesses and is arrested. But Jenufa and Laca go away to begin a new life together.

(CZECK)

Schwanda	Weinberger
(The Bagpiper)	(1896-)

Première: Prague, 1927.
Première: New York, Metropolitan Opera House,
      1931, with Maria Müller as Dorota, Friedrich
      Schorr as Schwanda, Karin Branzell as the Queen,
      Rudolf Laubenthal as Babinsky, Gustave Schut-
      zendorf as the devil.
Gay folk opera in two acts and five scenes.
Book by Milos Kares; translated and arranged by Max
      Brod.
Action: Schwanda's farmyard. Queen Ice-Heart's pal-
      ace. The old story of music's charms.

185

Dorota, wife of the bagpiper, Schwanda, has attracted Babinsky, chief of the robbers, and he determines to have her for his own. To get Schwanda out of the way, he takes him out into the world with his bagpipe. Dorota follows. Schwanda's music so pleases the Queen Ice-Heart that she offers him marriage. But Dorota appears and the angry Queen orders Schwanda beheaded. His music, however, makes all the court dance back into the city and the gate is locked. Schwanda tells Dorota that the devil may take him if he has kissed the Queen. The devil appears and Schwanda is taken to hell. Babinsky rescues him by playing a game of cards with the devil, and restores him to his wife, Dorota. Babinsky goes sadly on his way.

(CZECK)

| *Spuk im Schloss* | Jaroslav Kricka |
| (The Ghost in the Castle) | (1882-   ) |

Première: Breslau, 1931.
Humorous opera based on a short story by Oscar Wilde. Modern America and Medieval Europe amusingly contrasted. Its musical form saves it from the light opera class.

Mr. and Mrs. Hollywood, an American couple, have rented a Bohemian castle which is supposed to be haunted. They take it for a week end with the idea of capturing the ghost and sending it back home to the museum of their mid-western town in the States. The Lord of the castle has told them that the ghost can be caught only by the kiss of an unafraid maiden. Eleanor, the beautiful daughter of the Hollywoods, is not afraid, so she meets the ghost and gives the expected kiss. The ghost proves to be the Lord of the castle, and when the marriage takes place everybody is pleased.

(CZECK)

Leuten von Poker-Flat   Weinberger
(People of Poker Flat)   (1896-   )

Première: Brunn, Moravia, 1932.
Music drama in nine pictures. Libretto by Kares, based
     on stories of Bret Harte.
Action: California, no definite period. Present day
     costumes. The gold-diggers watch movies and
     listen to jazz.

Among the gold-diggers in a mining camp is John Hamlin, a recluse and a skeptic, very attractive to women but totally indifferent to them. A mail coach is attacked and the driver killed. A man whose land is wanted by the sheriff, is found guilty and sentenced to be hanged. All undesirables are made to leave the camp, among them being Hamlin. They leave, their way lying through the mountains where they suffer from cold and hunger. Hamlin is indifferent to the advances of a woman who loves him; indifferent to the death of the man who was innocent of the mail coach robbery; does not protest at being put out of the camp. Many die of exhaustion, cold, lack of food. Hamlin, rather than ask help, shoots himself.

187

Slavic

Honzova Kralovstvi   Otaker Ostrcil
(Hans' Kingdom)   (1879-1936)

Première: Prague, 1935. (Previous hearings in Bruenn
    and Maerisch-Ostrau)
Music drama in three acts, with prologue and epilogue.
    Libretto by J. Maranek.
Story freely adapted from a Tolstoy fairy tale.

Satan comes to earth to see what trouble he can make
in a little peaceful village. Here he finds an old peasant
who has three sons—one, Hans, peace-loving and kind;
another, a merchant, not too honest, and one, a fiery-
tempered soldier. Under the devil's influence these two
bad brothers try to bring disaster to Hans, who through
kindness and charity disarms the devil's designs. The Devil
becomes disgusted and goes back home to his fire and
brimstone.

Zar Kalojan   Pantscho Wladigeroff
                      (1899-   )

Première: Bratislava-on-the-Danube (in prewar days
    the Hungarian Pressburg), 1937.
A tragic music drama in three acts.
Libretto by Nicolai Liliev and Fany Popova-Mutafova.
Action: Bulgaria, first part of thirteenth century—the
    period of the Crusades. A chapter in Bulgarian
    history.

In the time of the Crusades, Kalojan is made Czar and wars against the Flemish Count Baldwin who poses as the Emperor of Rome. Czar Kalojan captures and imprisons Baldwin but treats him with deference. Czarina Maria falls in love with Baldwin but when he refuses to listen to her love-making she, in revenge, tells her husband that Baldwin is making improper advances to her. In a mad rage Kalojan kills the innocent man and Maria commits suicide.

(CROATIAN)

Mirjana   Josef Mandic
                                              (1883-   )
Première: Olmutz, 1937.
Tragic mystical opera in three acts.
Story based on a Slavic legend, in the belief of no physical death.

Mirjana, a young peasant girl, falls ill and dies in her lover's arms, making him promise that if he marries another, he and the wedding procession will pass by her grave. He keeps his promise—stops the procession, leaving his friends to wait for him, descends to her grave. When he returns no one is there. He has been gone a hundred years. He meets the Countess Mira and thinks she is Mirjana. They go away together and her lover follows. He murders the lover and is finally united in spirit to his first love, Mirjana.

NOTE: The critic, Max Brod, thinks it will "surpass *Schwanda* in popularity."

189

Slavic

Wallenstein   Weinberger
                                               (1896-   )

Première: Vienna, 1937.
Lyric tragedy in six scenes or episodes.
Story based on the Schiller tragedy. Libretto by Milos
    Kares, who skillfully reduced this immense trilogy
    of eleven acts into six scenes.
Action: Bohemia, time of the Thirty Years' War.

Wallenstein, commander of the German Emperor's
forces, has been planning to desert the Emperor when he
finds a betrayer among his own generals, the one he trusted
most, Octavio Piccolomini. Thekla, daughter of Wallenstein, and Max, son of the treacherous general, love each
other. After a love scene in which eternal fidelity is sworn,
Max leaves for the scene of war. Wallenstein finds himself
deserted by many of his regiments. Max is killed in a des-
perate attack. Wallenstein is lured to the border of Bohemia and is murdered by his own generals.

(BOHEMIAN)

Alfred   Anton Dvorak
                                            (1841-1904)

Première: Prague, 1938.
Heroic opera in three acts.
Story after a play by Theodor Koerner.
Action: England, about the fifth century.

AT HOME AND ABROAD
Slavic

Harold, a Danish chieftain, defeats the Britons in battle. He falls in love with Alwine, bride of Alfred, King of Britain, and when she repulses him, imprisons her in a tower. Alfred disguises himself as a harper and gains entrance to the tower, but is discovered. A battle follows between the Danes and the Britons in which the Britons are victorious. The Danes flee and Harold kills himself.

NOTE: This opera was written when the composer was 29 years old. He was at that time an unknown player in the orchestra of the National Theatre in Prague. The opera was never before produced until February, 1938, when it was given in abbreviated form as a broadcast from Prague on that date

SLAVIC OPERA

(Polish, Czeck, Bulgarian,
Croatian, Bohemian)

(PART II)

composed *before 1900*, and

presented *for the first time in the*

United States during the

*XX*TH *Century*

(in prominent Opera Houses), also

Outstanding Revivals in the United

States during the same period.

1900 — Season 1937–1938

(inclusive)

(BOHEMIAN)

The Bartered Bride   Smetana
                                      (1824-1884)

Première: Prague, 1866.
Première: New York, Metropolitan Opera House,
        1909, with Emmy Destinn as Marie, Carl Jorn as
        Hans, Adamo Didur as Kezal, Albert Reiss as
        Wenzel.
        Revival, Metropolitan Opera House, 1933,
        with Elizabeth Rethberg as Marie, Rudolf Laub-
        enthal as Hans, Ludwig Hoffmann as Kezal, Marek
        Windham as Wenzel.
Comedy opera in three acts.
Text by K. Sabina.
Action: Slavonic village, nineteenth century.

The parents of the lovely Marie, persuaded by the
marriage broker, Kezal, wish her to marry Wenzel, the
half-witted son of Micha. But Marie is in love with Hans,
a newcomer to the village, and the lovers are in despair.
Hans is finally persuaded to sell his claim on Marie to the
marriage broker for 200 ducats, with the condition that
she marry Micha's son. Marie cannot understand this action while Hans still insists that he loves her. The agree-
ment is signed and the villagers are present. Hans springs
a great surprise when he announces that he is the son of
Micha! It is revealed that he is, by a former marriage! All

193

ends happily, as Wenzel has fallen in love with a tight-rope walker with a travelling circus troupe which is in town. Hans and Marie are married, their parents bless them, and they begin housekeeping with the ducats paid by the marriage broker, who is the only loser.

NOTE: Smetana was the founder of the Bohemian National School. This is his best known opera.

SPANISH OPERA

composed and produced

abroad, in the United States, or

in both, during the

*XX*TH *Century*

1900 — Season 1937-1938

(inclusive)

Character of Spanish Opera

The folk music of Spain has greatly influenced Spanish composers, and also foreign composers. Syncopation is characteristic of Spanish music.

195

Spanish

La Vida Breve   Manuel de Falla
(A Brief Life)   (1877-   )

Première: Nice, 1913.
Première: New York, Metropolitan Opera House,
      1926, with Lucrezia Bori as Salud, Kathleen
      Howard as the Grandmother, Mere Alcock as
      Carmela, Armand Tokyatan as Paco, Louis D'An-
      gelo as Uncle Sarvaov.
Tragic opera in two acts, and four scenes. Book by
      Fernandes Shaw. Story of a gypsy maid of
      Granada.
Action: Granada, twentieth century.

   In the Gypsy quarter of Granada lives the lovely young
Gypsy, Salud. Her love has been won by Paco, who is
above her in station but who vows undying devotion.
Salud loves and trusts him. Her uncle, Sarvaov, has learned
that Paco is to marry the wealthy Carmela. When he discovers Salud in the arms of Paco he is about to kill Paco
but holds back. He cannot break the heart of little Salud.
The betrothal of Paco and Carmela is being celebrated
in Carmela's home. Little Salud, her uncle and her grandmother sing beneath the window. Paco listens with a
guilty conscience. The Gypsies enter. Salud tells the guests
that Paco has betrayed and deserted her. Paco denies her
statements. Salud cries, "Paco!" and falls dead at his feet.

Goyescas	Enrique Granados
(Rival Lovers)	(1867-1916)

Première: New York, Metropolitan Opera House,
    1916 (World Première), with Anna Fitziu as
    Rosario, Martinelli as Don Fernando, Perini as
    Pepa, de Luca as Paquiro.
Tragic opera in three acts.
Book by Periquet.
Action: Madrid, 1801.

Paquiro the bull fighter, is the lover of Pepa. Rosario,
a lady of the Court, is to marry Don Fernando. Pepa and
Don Fernando overhear Paquiro invite Rosario to attend
a candlelight ball, a rather questionable affair. Pepa and
Don Fernando both become jealous and Don Fernando
declares that he will take his lady to the ball himself! At
the ball Fernando and Paquiro quarrel. They agree to
fight, and Rosario and Fernando leave. In Rosario's garden
Fernando suddenly disappears. A cry is heard and Rosario
rushes into the darkness. She returns with her wounded
lover who dies in her arms.

ENGLISH OPERA

composed and produced

abroad, in the United States,

or in both, in the

*XX*TH *Century*

1900 — Season 1937-1938

(inclusive)

Character of English Opera

English Opera developed from the Masque, upon which were engrafted Italian ideas. With the advent, however, of the Ballad Opera—which style prevailed for a long period—the Italian influence was temporarily destroyed. Henry Purcell composed the first *pure* English opera, *Dido and Æneas*. Since the days of Ballad Opera, English Opera has advanced to a high standard, reflecting distinct style.

Much Ado About Nothing   Stanford
                                            (1852-1924)

Première: London, 1901.
Comedy opera in three acts.
After Shakespeare's play.

   Don Juan attempts to make Claudio believe that his
beloved, Hero, is unfaithful. The trick is exposed by the
confession of the villain, Borachio, who was in the pay of
Don Juan, and the two lovers are happily united.

Shamus O'Brien   Stanford
                                            (1852-1924)
Première: Breslau, Germany, 1907.
Pastoral opera in three acts.
Action: A village in Ireland, end of eighteenth century.

   Shamus O'Brien rebels against English laws. A spy betrays him and he is sentenced to be hanged. Through the
aid of a priest he escapes and the fire of the bullets with
which he is pursued kills the spy who had betrayed him.

A Village Romeo and Juliet   Frederick Delius
                                            (1863-1934)
Première: Berlin, 1907.
Première: London, 1920.
Impressionistic tragic opera in three (or four) acts.
Book after Kellar's *Folk of Sedvilla*.

English

Sali (the village Romeo) and Vrenchen (his Juliet) love each other although their fathers are enemies. They leave home and prefer death together while life is pure and lovely. They find a barge on the river and climb aboard. The barge sinks.

The Critic   Stanford
                                                (1852-1924)

Première: London, 1916.
Comedy opera in three acts.

The story is after Sheridan's play of the same title, with the sub-title; *A Tragedy Rehearsed*. As the play is a satire on the contemporary stage in Sheridan's time, this opera is a travesty on old Italian opera style. The characters include the Author, the Critic, and the Promoter.

The Immortal Hour   Rutland Boughton
                                          (1878-   )

Première: Glastonbury, 1916.
Symbolic opera in two acts.
Book after play by Fiona McCleod.

Eochaid, the young King of Irin, weds a fairy princess, Etain. Midir, Etain's fairy lover, breaks in on their immortal hour of happiness and leads Etain away. Eochaid cries out despairingly. Dalua, Lord of the Hidden Way says, "Nothing is left but the dream of death." The earthly must yield to the heavenly.

Koanga   Delius
                                      (1863-1934)

Première: Epilogue only, London, 1922.
Première: London, 1936, complete opera.
Text by Keary. Story after George Cable's *The Grandissimes*.
Action: Louisiana, early nineteenth century.

The story is one of Creole life in Louisiana in the early days of the nineteenth century and is supposed to be told by an old negro. It is a story of love and suffering told in an impersonal, narrative vein, as though unfolded by a commentator who reports each scene as it is enacted, but does not really live it.

The Seal Woman   Sir Granville Bantock
                                      (1868-   )

Première: Birmingham, England, 1924.
Celtic folk opera in two acts.
Book by Mrs. Kennedy-Fraser.
Action: Hebrides. Any time. A tragi-romantic tale.

The Seal Woman is a beautiful maid who wears a magic seal robe. Isleman, a young fisherman, is in love with her, but she is torn between the wish to be with him and her love of the wild life of the sea. Isleman seizes her magic robe and refuses to give it back. She yields and goes with him as his wife. After seven years, her child one day finds the seal robe. She snatches it from him, wraps herself in it and plunges into the sea never to return. Isleman appears too late and he sadly embraces the boy, now his all.

The Traveling Companion	Stanford
	(1852-1924)

Première: Liverpool, 1925.
Romantic fairy opera in four acts. Text by Newbolt.
Story after Hans Andersen's fairy tale.

During a storm John takes refuge in a church. A dead man lies there awaiting burial. Two robbers enter and begin to rob the corpse. John frightens them away. John learns that the Princess will wed the man who guesses her riddle. When he arrives at the palace he is given twenty-four hours to answer the riddle, which is to tell the Princess the thought in her mind. A mysterious traveling companion, befriended by John, tells him everything will be well. The Princess is under the power of a wizard. She asks him what to fix her mind upon and he replies that she shall think of his head. The traveling companion, who has, without her knowledge accompanied her to the wizard's cave, cuts off the wizard's head after she leaves. The next day when the Princess asks the question, John produces the wizard's head. Thus the Princess is freed from the wizard's power. The traveling companion proves to be the dead man whom John had saved from the robbers and thus he pays his debt of gratitude, then disappears.

Queen of Cornwall	Boughton
	(1878-)

Première: London, 1924.
Legendary tragic opera in three acts.
Book after Thomas Hardy's poem.
Action: Ancient Britain. A version of the Tristan legend.

Iseult of the White Hands requests the Queen, wife of King Mark, to go to the dying Tristan and nurse him back to life. Tristan recovers when he hears of her coming. He hastens to the castle disguised as a minstrel and is killed by King Mark in a fit of jealousy. The Queen kills her husband and throws herself over a cliff.

The Alchemist	Cyril Scott
	(1879-)

Première: Essen, 1925.
Symbolic opera in three acts.
Text by composer.
Action: Medieval times.

A youth begs the sage for the magic spell that will give him his heart's desire, gold. Following the bidding of the sage the youth is terrified at the pile of heaped up treasure and rushes back to the feet of the sage, who tells him that the secret of happiness lies within the soul and not in gold. The youth begs to be taught this that happiness may be his now. "The secret of happiness lies within one's self."

English

Hugh the Drover   Vaughan-Williams
                                               (1872-   )
Première: London, 1925.
Première: Washington, D. C., 1928 (United States
    Première) with Tudor Davies (who created the
    role in England) as Hugh, Marie Montana (Ameri-
    can debut) as Mary the Constable's daughter, Ivan
    Ivantzoff as John the Butcher, Alfred Valenti as
    the Constable. Eugene Goosens, friend of the com-
    poser, conducted.
Romantic folk opera in two acts. Text by Harold Child.
Action: Small town in Cotswold Hills about 1812.

John, the Butcher, betrothed to Mary, who does not
love him, is thrusting his attentions upon her at the fair
when Hugh the Drover appears and he and Mary fall in
love. It is agreed that Hugh and John shall fight, the best
man winning the lady. Hugh comes out victor, but Mary's
father, the Constable, arrests Hugh as a French spy. The
next morning Mary joins Hugh in the stocks. A sergeant
in command of a squad enters and recognizing Hugh as
an old friend, secures his release. Mary leaves with him in
spite of her father's opposition.

At the Boar's Head   Gustave Holst
                                               (1874-1934)
Première: London, 1925.
Première: New York, MacDowell Club Auditorium,
    1935, with John Gurney as Falstaff, Kurt Brown-
    ell as Prince Harry, Marion Selee as Doll Tear-
    sheet.

Folk opera in one act.
Tale after Shakespeare.
Action: Old London, Boar's Head Inn.

Drinking and carousing at the Boar's Head Inn in Old London, Prince Harry has just received word that his father awaits him at Westminster. He decides to give up his dissolute life and join his father at the wars. Inspired by the thrilling war march, *Lord Willoughby*, which is heard outside, he seizes his sword and cloak and dashes out, leaving the fat old knight Falstaff behind. However, Falstaff hastens to follow much to the sorrow of Doll Tearsheet.

Judith   Goosens
                                          (1893-   )
Première: London, 1928.
Première: Philadelphia, 1929, (American Première) by Philadelphia Opera Company, with Bianca Saroya as Judith, Ivan Steschenko as Holofernes, Carol Ault as Achoir. Conducted by the composer.
Sacred opera in one act.
Libretto by Arnold Bennett, after the Biblical story from the Apocryphal book of Judith.
Action: Biblical times.

Holofernes, enemy of the Jews and commander of the Assyrians, is laying siege to Bethulia. He captures and binds Achoir, a captain of the Jews. Judith, a beautiful Jewess, cuts the bonds of Achoir and to save her people goes to the tent of Holofernes. He becomes so infatuated

205

English

with her charms and beauty that he arranges a banquet in her honor. Before the feast she has her servant hide a scimitar in the tent. She drugs Holofernes' wine and when he sinks into a drunken stupor she beheads him and returns to the camp at Bethulia with his head. When the Jews see it they fall upon the Assyrians and defeat them.

The Song of Songs   Bantock
                                                       (1868-   )

Première: Manchester, England, 1930.
Sacred opera in five acts.
Biblical text from the Song of Solomon.

Don Juan de Manara   Goosens
                                                       (1893-   )

Première: London, 1937, with the celebrated American baritone, Lawrence Tibbett in the title role.
Lyric drama in four acts.
Libretto by Arnold Bennett after his play of the same name.
Action: Castile, Spain, sixteenth century.

Don Juan is giving a supper party in the castle of his father, the Duke, who is dying and is about to make Jose, illegitimate brother of Don Juan, heir to the estate. Don Juan has sent a priest to influence his father in his favor but the priest has failed and Don Juan kills him. Don Juan visits Dona Inez in her boudoir. Jose follows but is beaten off by Juan's orders. Don Juan carries Inez off to Madrid and Jose kills himself. Don Juan, in a card game with Don Luis, wins from him his mistress, Paquita, but she will not yield while Luis lives, so Don Juan kills him. Paquita poisons herself. She begs Don Juan to go to her sister Marta, who is a nun in a convent, and beg her to pray for her soul. While Don Juan is giving the message to Marta, the ghost of Jose appears, disarms Don Juan but tells him his life will be spared if he finds one pure woman who will give her life for his. Marta offers her life but Don Juan, full of remorse and desiring to atone, becomes a priest.

AMERICAN OPERA

composed and produced

during the

XXTH *Century*

1900 — Season 1937-1938

(inclusive)

With the exception of two, American
Operas in this period had their World
Premières in the United States.

Character of American Opera

American Opera embodies the principles and form of
opera in general, and is fast developing its own distinct
style.

XXth CENTURY OPERA

American

The Pipe of Desire	Frederick S. Converse
	(1871-)

Première: Boston, 1906.
Première: New York, Metropolitan Opera Company,
    at New Theatre, 1910, with Ricardo Martin as
    Iolan, Louise Homer as Naoia.
Romantic opera in one act.
Book by George E. Barton.
A symbolic tale. The first American opera produced
    at the Metropolitan Opera House.

   Iolan, a peasant youth, dares to play the magic pipe
though the Elf King of the forest tells him that its playing
is death to mortals. He is full of joy for he is to marry
Naoia tomorrow. He visions his rose-bound cottage, wife
and children greeting him. He calls his wife. She comes,
but only to die in his arms, for the magic pipe music has
brought her death. Iolan curses, but the Elf King takes the
pipe and the youth passes away.

NOTE: The New Theatre was at this time used regularly by the
Metropolitan Company.

The Sacrifice	Converse
	(1871-)

Première: Boston, 1911, with Alice Nielson as Chonita,
    Constantino as Bernal, Raman Blanchart as Burton.
Tragic opera in three acts. Libretto by the composer.
Story from a tale, *Dolores,* by Lieut. Wise, U. S. A.

209

Action: Coast of California, 1846.

During the Mexican War, Bernal, a Mexican officer sees and loves Chonita. He has to cross the Mexican line to see her and is jealous of Burton, an American captain, who also loves her. Bernal is wounded and Chonita hides him in the Mission occupied by the Americans. In a delirium he rushes out and is arrested as a spy. Burton realizes that the girl loves Bernal, but he is too honorable to let his prisoner escape. However, a sudden attack by the Mexicans presents a chance to prove his love for Chonita. He exposes himself to the Mexican bullets and is killed. The lovers realize that he sacrificed his life for their happiness.

Natoma   Victor Herbert
                                           (1859-1924)

Première: Philadelphia, 1911, with Mary Garden as
     Natoma, John McCormack as Paul, Lillian Gren-
     ville as Barbara, Sammarco as Alvarado, Huber-
     deau as Don Francisco.
Première: New York, Metropolitan Opera House,
     1911, with same cast.
Tragi-romantic opera in three acts. Book by J. D.
     Redding.
Action: California under Spanish rule, 1820.

Natoma, a beautiful Indian girl, is in love with Paul Merrill, an officer of the United States Navy. Paul loves

Barbara, daughter of Don Francisco. Natoma saves Barbara from abduction by Alvarado, by burying her dagger in Alvarado's heart. She takes refuge in the church. Realizing the hopelessness of her love for Paul she decides to become a nun.

Mona   Horatio Parker
                          (1863-1919)

Première: New York, Metropolitan Opera House,
     1912, with Louise Homer as Mona, Ricardo Martin as Gwynn, Putnam Griswold as the Roman Governor.
Tragic opera in three acts. Book by Brian Hooker.
Action: Old Britain, time of the Druids. A partly mythical story.

In Druid Britain, Mona, Princess of Britain, plans war against the Roman invaders. Gwynn, whose father is a Roman and his mother a Briton, wishes to reconcile the two nations and win Mona, whom he loves. Mona loves him but does not trust him and takes him captive. When the Romans win the war, Gwynn escapes. He sees Mona and begs her to listen to his plan, but she denounces him as a traitor and slays him. When the Roman Governor comes he recognizes the dead Gwynn as his son. Mona is led away into captivity.

211

XXth CENTURY OPERA
American

Cyrano de Bergerac　　　　　Walter Damrosch
　　　　　　　　　　　　　　　　(1862-　　)

Première: New York, Metropolitan Opera House,
　　　1913, with Frances Alda as Roxanne, Ricardo
　　　Martin as Christian, Pasquale Amata as Cyrano.
Tragic opera in four acts. Libretto by W. J. Hender-
　　　son. Story after Edmond Rostand's drama. (*Sword
　　　and Cloak romance*).
Action: Paris and environs, 1640.

Cyrano of the huge nose is hopelessly in love with his
cousin Roxanne. He learns that Roxanne loves Christian,
his friend. Christian is however unable to write sonnets
and love-letters and is slow of speech. Cyrano composes
poems and sonnets and writes the love letters signing his
friend's name. Christian wins Roxanne. Many years later
the truth comes out, when Cyrano is mortally wounded,
Christian having fallen in battle.

Madeleine　　　　　　　　　Victor Herbert
　　　　　　　　　　　　　　　(1859-1924)

Première: New York, Metropolitan Opera House,
　　　1914, with Frances Alda as Madeleine, Paul Alt-
　　　house as Francois, Duc d'Esterre, Leonora Sparkes
　　　as Nichette the maid, de Segurola as Didier, Pini
　　　Corsi as Chevalier de Mauprat.
Lyric drama in one act,

AT HOME AND ABROAD

American

Book by Grant Stewartl
Action: Paris home of Madeleine. New Year's Eve,
    1770.

Madeleine, a very lovely opera singer, has several devoted admirers, among them Didier, an artist, the Chevalier de Mauprat and the Duc d'Esterre. When none of
these finds it possible to dine with her on New Year's Day
"because he is to dine with his mother," she after all has
the company of one dearest to her heart, when she places
her mother's picture opposite to her at the table, thus
"dining with her mother."

Fairyland   Horatio Parker
                                         (1863-1919)

Première: Los Angeles, 1915, with Marcella Craft as
    Rosamond, Ralph Errolle as King Auburn, Wm.
    Wade Hinshaw as Cowain the King's brother,
    Kathleen Howard as the Abbess.
Allegorical opera in three acts.
Libretto by Brian Hooker.
Action: In the mountains somewhere in Europe, early
    fourteenth century.

Rosamond, a novice, is to be burned at the stake because
she has not kept her church vows. Her lover, King
Auburn, is with her. They have had many mysterious
adventures that discredit the accepted rules of church and
state. A great sense of pity fills Rosamond's heart and the

213

scene is transformed. Nuns and soldiers flee as faggots are extinguished and chains drop off. The lovers mount the fairy throne and all the people turn to fairies and all is happiness.

The Canterbury Pilgrims   DeKoven
                                                 (1859-1920)

Première: New York, Metropolitan Opera House, 1917, with Johannes Sembach as Chaucer, Margaret Ober as the Wife of Bath, Edith Mason as the Prioress, Albert Reiss as King Richard.
Romantic folk-opera in four acts.
Book by Percy Mackaye after Chaucer's *Canterbury Tales*.
Action: Britain, 1383.

On the road to the shrine of Thomas á Becket at Canterbury, the Wife of Bath, five times a widow, plans to make the poet Chaucer her sixth husband. However, Chaucer is in love with the gentle Prioress. The Wife of Bath leads Chaucer to make a wager that she cannot obtain a certain jewel from the Prioress, with the understanding that if she does procure the jewel Chaucer will marry her as she wishes. She does obtain the jewel, by trickery, but the King decrees that the sixth husband of the Wife of Bath shall be the Miller. This brings joy to the lovers and all is well.

Azora   Henry Hadley
                                            (1871-1937)

Première: Chicago, 1917, Chicago Opera Association
    (World Première), with Anna Fitziu as Azora,
    Forrest Lamont as Prince Xalea, Arthur Middle-
    ton as Ramatzin, Frank Preisch as Canek, James
    Goddard as Montezuma.
Première: New York, 1918, Lexington Theatre with
    same company.
Tragic opera in three acts.
Action: Mexico in the time of Montezuma, 1479-1520.

Azora, daughter of Montezuma, and Prince Xalca love
each other. Canek the High Priest advises Xalca to give
up hope of marrying Azora, but the lovers pledge eternal
devotion. Xalca wins a battle for which Montezuma has
promised any reward he may desire. He asks for Azora.
Montezuma becomes furious and condemns them both
to death, but will spare Azora if she will wed Ramatzin
the Aztec general. She refuses and she and her lover are
about to be sacrificed when Cortez and his soldiers appear
and as the cross they carry gleams in the sunlight, Canek's
dagger falls from his hand and he faints in terror. The
power of the Christian faith is felt by all and praises to
God are sung.

Shanewis   Charles W. Cadman
                                            (1881-   )

Première: New York, Metropolitan Opera House,
    1918, with Sophie Braslau as Shanewis, Paul Alt-

215

house as Lionel, Thomas Chalmers as Philip, Kathleen Howard as Mrs. Everton, Marie Sundelius as Amy Everton.
Tragic opera in two acts.
Book by Nelle Richmond Eberhard.
Action: California and Oklahoma, 1911.

Shanewis, an Indian girl, is a protege of Mrs. Everton. When Amy Everton returns from Europe her mother gives a reception and has Shanewis sing in her Indian costume. Lionel, Amy's betrothed, becomes infatuated with Shanewis who knows nothing of his engagement to Amy. When he asks her to marry him she tells him that he must ask her people. While they are at the Indian Reservation Mrs. Everton and Amy drive up and when the state of affairs is explained Amy is shocked at the treachery of Lionel. Shanewis curses Lionel and orders him to leave. But the young Indian, Philip, who loves Shanewis, pierces Lionel's heart with a poisoned arrow and Shanewis cries, "In death he is mine!"

The Legend   Joseph Carl Briel
                                                 (1870-1926)

Première: New York, Metropolitan Opera House, 1919, with Paul Althouse as Stephen, Rosa Ponselle as Carmelita, Louis d'Angelo as the Count.
Tragic opera in one act.
Libretto by Jacques Byrne.

216

Action: Muscovadia, a mythical country of the Balkans. A stormy night.

Carmelita, daughter of Count Stackareff, has a lover, Stephen. Stephen is on the trail of the Count—commissioned to arrest him as a bandit, for it has been discovered that the Count is a gentleman by day and bandit by night. Carmelita and Stephen are about to elope when her father, the Count, enters. When Stephen tells him he is hunting a bandit the Count rushes out. Stephen goes after him but Carmelita calls him back and plunges a dagger into his heart. The soldiers bring in the body of the Count whom they have shot and finding Stephen dead, they shoot Carmelita.

The Temple Dancer   John Adam Hugo
                                    (1873-   )
Première: New York, Metropolitan Opera House,
        1919, with Florence Easton as the Temple Dancer,
        Morgan Kingston as the Temple Guard.
Tragic opera in one act.
Book by Mme. Jutta Bell-Ranske.
Action: Hindoo Temple of Mahadeo.

A Hindoo girl curses her gods because they will not help her in her love affairs. She is told she must die but she continues her curses, poisons her jailer, and while she is stealing jewels from the temple she is killed by a bolt of lightning.

American

Rip van Winkle   Reginald deKoven
                                        (1859-1920)

Première: Chicago, 1920, Chicago Opera Association
    (World Première), with Evelyn Herbert as Pet-
    erkee, Edna Darch as Katrina, George Baklanoff
    as Rip van Winkle, Hector Dufranne as Henrik
    Hudson, Huberdeau as Vedder.
Première: New York, (first time) Lexington Theatre,
    1920, with same cast.
Comedy opera in three acts. Libretto by Percy Mac-
    kaye. Story after Irving's legend.
Action: A Dutch village in the Catskills.

It is the wedding-day of Katrina of the sharp tongue,
and Rip van Winkle. But the bridegroom forgets about
it and goes fishing with Peterkee, Katrina's little sister.
Henrik Hudson's ghost appears and takes Rip off for a
game of bowls with him. He gives Rip a magic drink and
he falls asleep. Twenty years pass and when Rip wakes up
and returns to the village he is an old man. Katrina is married and has a family. Peterkee has kept Hudson's magic
flask and gives Rip a drink. He becomes a young man
again and marries Peterkee.

Cleopatra's Night   Henry Hadley
                                        (1871-   )

Première: New York, Metropolitan Opera House,
    1920, with Frances Alda as Cleopatra, Orville
    Harrold as Meiamoun, Jeanne Gordon as Mardion.

Tragic opera in two acts. Book by Alice L. Pollack. Story after Gautier's *Une Nuit de Cleopatre.* Action: Egypt at the time of Cleopatra.

Cleopatra is about to step into her bath when an arrow bearing the message, "I love you," falls at her feet and very soon the head of an Egyptian lad appears above the water. It is Meiamoun, whom Mardion, Cleopatra's maid loves, and he has swum through the conduit from the Nile. He has sent the message to Cleopatra who consents to let him spend one night in her tent but he is to die the next morning. Mardion hears this and kills herself. In the morning the poison is given and the boy falls dead at Cleopatra's feet. Just then the arrival of Marc Antony is announced and Cleopatra rises to greet him with a kiss.

The Witch of Salem   Cadman
                                                            (1881-   )

Première: Chicago, Chicago Civic Opera Association, season 1926-27 (World Première) with Irene Pavloska as Sheila, Eide Norena as Claris, Charles Hackett as Arnold Talbot.
Lyric drama in one act. Book by Nellie Richmond Eberhard. A tale of religious hysteria in early Puritan days.
Action: Salem Village, Mass., about 1692.

Sheila, ward of Willoughby, is in love with Arnold Talbot, who, however, loves Willoughby's daughter, Claris.

219

Around the fireside there is much talk of witches and the young sister of Claris innocently mentions the red mark on Claris' breast. Later, Sheila reminds Talbot that he once kissed her and that she loves him. But he cannot return her love, and, angry with jealousy she plans to have Claris accused of being a witch because of the red mark on her breast. When Claris is accused and her dress torn apart the red mark is seen and she is thrown into prison. When she is on her way to be hung as a witch, Sheila confesses and she is put to death instead of Claris.

Namiko-San   Aldo Franchetti
                                              (1883-   )

Première: Chicago, 1925 (World Première), Chicago
    Civic Opera Association, with Tamika Miura as
    Namiko-San, Richard Bonelli as Yiro, the Warrior
    Prince, Theodore Rich as Yasui, a young monk.
    Conducted by the composer.
Lyric drama in one act. Libretto by the composer.
    Story after Leo Duran's translation from *An
    Ancient Japanese Tragedy.*
Action: Medieval Japan.

The lovely Namiko-San, betrothed to the Prince, is in the woods gathering flowers when she meets a young monk and a mutual love springs in their hearts. The Prince finds them together that night and is about to plunge his sword into the breast of the monk when Namiko-San throws herself upon the sword. The Prince is filled with sorrow and remorse when he finds that little Namiko-San was innocent of wrong.

NOTE: The composer is a naturalized American citizen. "At the close of the Première, the Bispham Memorial Medal was bestowed on the composer by the American Opera Society of Chicago."

Castle Agrazant   Ralph Lyford
                                          (1882-1927)

Première: Cincinnati, 1926, with Olga Forrai as Isa-
    beau, Forrest Lamont as Richard, Howard Preston
    as Geoffrey. Composer conducted.
Tragic opera in three acts.
Libretto by the composer.
Action: Medieval France, after the last Crusade.

Richard of Agrazant returns from the Crusades to find his wife missing, and in the cradle of her dead baby a note which tells that she has been carried off by Geoffrey of Lisiac. Richard declares vengeance and, disguised as a monk, enters Geoffrey's castle and kills him, but not before Geoffrey mortally wounds Isabeau. Richard realizes all too late that he should have stayed at home, insuring the safety of his wife and child rather than following the Crusaders. He breaks his sword.

221

American

The King's Henchman	Deems Taylor
	(1885-)

Première: New York, Metropolitan Opera House,
    1927, with Florence Easton as Aelfrida, Edward
    Johnson as Aethelwold, Lawrence Tibbett as Ead-
    gar.
Tri-romantic opera in three acts. Libretto by Edna St.
    Vincent Millay. Story based on a Halloween
    legend.
Action: West England, tenth century.

King Eadgar has heard of the beautiful Aelfrida, daughter of Ordgar of Devon. He sends his young and handsome friend, Aethelwold, to find out whether she will
make a suitable Queen. Aethelwold, heretofore indifferent to women, falls in love with Aelfrida himself and sends
word to the King that she is not at all suited to be Queen
as she is ugly. However, he says, since Aelfrida's father
is rich and he, Aethelwold, is poor, he asks the King's
blessing on his marriage to Aelfrida. They are married.
One day King Eadgar arrives. Aethelwold tells his wife
of the deception which he has committed and tells her to
go to bed and pretend an illness. Instead, she decks herself
in a rich robe and in all her dazzling beauty she greets the
King. The King at once senses the falsehood of his friend,
and Aethelwold, in remorse, stabs himself. King Eadgar
mourns his beloved friend, and the penitent Aelfrida falls
at the foot of the cross.

AT HOME AND ABROAD

Peter Ibbetson   Deems Taylor
                                                          (1885-   )

Première: New York, Metropolitan Opera House,
    1931, with Lucrezia Bori as the Duchess of Tow-
    ers (Mimsey), Edward Johnson as Peter Ibbetson,
    Lawrence Tibbett as Col. Ibbetson.
Tragic opera in three acts. Libretto by Constance Col-
    lier and the composer. Story after Du Maurier's
    novel.
Action: Paris and England, nineteenth century.

    Peter Ibbetson had an ideal childhood in Paris. Mimsey
was one of his playmates and he loved her dearly. Circumstances take him to England where the cold English climate
and environment make him long for his early home. He
meets Mimsey grown to womanhood and now the stately
and beautiful Duchess of Towers. Their love is hopeless.
When Peter's uncle, Col. Ibbetson, declares that Peter is
an illegitimate child Peter kills him and is sent to prison
for life. His one consolation is "dreaming true" with his
beloved Mimsey as his life fades out.

Jack and the Beanstalk   Louis Gruenberg
                                                          (1883-   )

Première: New York, Juilliard Opera School, 1931,
    with Beatrice Heght as the Mother, Mary Atkins
    as Jack, Ruby Mercer as the Princess, Julius
    Huehn as the Giant.

223

Fairy opera in three acts, thirteen scenes.
Libretto by John Erskine.
Play after the fairy story of the same name, which
incidents it follows.

Caponsacchi	Richard Hagemann
(Tragedy in Arezzo)	(1882-)

Première: Frieburg, 1932.
Première: Vienna, 1935.
Première: New York, Metropolitan Opera House,
    1937, with Helen Jepson as Pompilia, Lawrence
    Tibbett as Caponsacchi, Mario Chamlee as Guido.
Tragic opera in three acts, with prologue and epilogue.
    Book by Arthur Goodrich. Story after Browning's
    Ring and the Book.
Action: Rome, Arezzo, Castelnuovo, last half of seven-
    teenth century.

Guido Francheschini, on trial before the Papal court for
the murder of his wife, Pompilia, and her parents claims
that he killed his wife for infidelity with the priest, Caponsacchi. Caponsacchi's defense proves that he rescued
the gentle Pompilia from the base cruelty of her husband
and carried her to Rome to await the birth of her lawful
child. The innocence of Pompilia and of Caponsacchi is
established and the sentence of death passed upon Guido.

Lucedia   Vittorio Giannini
                                              (1903-   )

Première: Munich, 1934.
Romantic opera in three acts, with prologue and six
    scenes. Libretto by G. M. Salac and Karl Flaster.
    Story styled *A Legend from Heathen Times* and
    resembles that of Spontini's *La Vestale*.

Lucedia, a vestal, is wooed by an adventurous youth
who pushes his way into the forest retreat of the virgin.
They are in each other's arms when discovered by the
High Priest. They are imprisoned and condemned to
death, being put to sea in a leaky boat.

Emperor Jones   Gruenberg
                                              (1883-   )

Première: New York, Metropolitan Opera House,
    1933, with Lawrence Tibbett as Brutus Jones,
    Mark Windham as Smithers a cockney trader.
Tragic opera in one act and seven scenes. Story adapted
    from Eugene O'Neill's play of the same name.
Action: West Indies, present time.

A fugitive from justice in the States, ex-Pullman porter
Brutus Jones has for two years ruled as Emperor on an
island in the West Indies. Learning from a cockney trader
that the people are about to revolt, Jones decides to flee
to the woods. He takes his revolver which contains six
bullets, one of which is silver, the only one that can kill

225

him, he says. In his flight he has visions of the man he killed in the States, of the guard he killed, each time shooting his pistol until all of the bullets are gone except the silver one. Finally the natives close in on him, and crying, "I'se your Emperor yet!" he shoots himself.

Helen Retires   George Antheil
                                                    (1900-   )

Première: New York, Juilliard Opera School, 1934, with alternating casts — Marvel Biddle and Martha Dwyer as Helen, Julius Huehn and George Britton as Achilles, Gean Greenwell and Roderic Cross as the Old Fisherman, Arthur Mahoney as the Young Fisherman.
Romantic comedy opera in three acts.
Text by John Erskine.
A travesty on the loves of "Helen of Troy."

After the passing of Menelaus, Helen sets out to find the love she has never known—Achilles. He is the one who will satisfy her longing. She visits the Island of the Blest where all shades dwell, there finds Achilles, and both repair to the Elysian Fields. They are joyously singing when an Old Fisherman, two sailors and a handsome Young Fisherman appear. They have come under the love spell of the song. The Old Fisherman wants to go home. In answer to Helen's question, "Does he love his wife?" he tells her that once he did but such love fades "like a flower." Helen lifts the spell and he leaves. She decides the old man is right and sends Achilles away at once "before the flower fades." She is now awaiting death but has taken pains to make her attire attractive. When the Young Fisherman, who is still under her spell, comes along, Helen, instead of dying decides she will live for him.

Merry Mount   Howard Hanson
                                                   (1896-   )

Première: Ann Arbor, Michigan, 1933, with John
    Charles Thomas as Wrestling Bradford, Leonora
    Corona as Lady Marigold, Frederick Jagel as Sir
    Gower. (This was in concert form, with the
    special permission of the Metropolitan Opera As-
    sociation, as it was to be given during the coming
    season by that organization.
Première: New York, Metropolitan Opera House,
    1934 (first performance of the work in operatic
    form), with Lawrence Tibbett as Wrestling Brad-
    ford, Gota Ljungberg as Lady Marigold, Edward
    Johnson as Sir Gower.
Lyric drama in four acts and five scenes. Text by R. L.
    Stokes. Story after Hawthorne's *Maypole of
    Merry Mount.*
Action: New England, Puritan days.

The tale deals with the conflict between Puritan and Cavalier colonists in early New England. Wrestling Brad- ford, a fanatical Puritan minister, becomes the victim of carnal love. He confesses to the elder of the church that in his dreams he is pursued by a beautiful woman who

American

tempts him to forget his religion. The elder suggests a
holy union with his daughter Plentiful. This is agreed upon
and their troth is plighted. Jack Prence is being whipped
by the Puritans for playing games with the children on
Sunday and is rescued by Lady Marigold, who is one of
the Cavaliers. Bradford recognizes her as the woman of his
dreams and stops the fighting between the Puritans and
the Cavaliers. He declares to the Lady his mad love for her
but she tells him she is to marry Sir Gower. Bradford
secretly plans to prevent this. The Cavaliers are having a
Maypole celebration, when the Puritans break up the
festivities, drive away the peaceful Indians who are looking on, carry Lady Marigold to the woods and imprison
Sir Gower. Bradford tells his love to Lady Marigold but
she resists him. Sir Gower, having freed himself, comes
to her aid and Bradford kills him. The angry Indians set
fire to the village. The Puritans are horrified when Bradford throws away his Bible and renounces his religion. He
brands Lady Marigold as a witch, drags her into the flames
with him and they both perish.

In the Pasha's Garden   J. L. Seymour
                                          (1894-   )

Première: New York, Metropolitan Opera House,
         1935, with Helen Jepson as Helene, Lawrence
         Tibbett as the Pasha, Marek Windham as Zumbul
         Agha, Frederick Jagel as Etienne.
Tragic opera in one act.

AT HOME AND ABROAD

English text by H. C. Tracy, after a tale by H. C. Dwight.

Action: Modern Constantinople.

The elderly Pasha's young wife, Helene, has a lover, Etienne. While they are in the garden together a servant approaches. Helene hurriedly hides Etienne in a chest. The servant becomes suspicious when Helene, from excitement, cannot lock the chest. As darkness falls the Pasha comes for a cup of tea. Helene quietly talks though filled with fear, but is somewhat reassured by the attitude of the Pasha. When she goes into the house she leaves the key. The Pasha locks the chest and has the servant dig a hole in the ground. They bury the chest and the Pasha throws the key into the well.

Gale

Ethel Leginska
(1890-   )

Première: Chicago, 1935, with John Charles Thomas as Gale, Frank Forest as Pascoe, Julia Peters as Jenifer. Conducted by composer.

Tragic opera in one act and three scenes. Libretto by the composer. Story after the novel, *The Haunting*, by the English authoress, Mrs. C. Dawson Smith.

Action: Seaport village in Cornwall, early nineteenth century.

In a seaport village in Cornwall live two brothers—Gale, the elder, sedate and steady, and Pascoe, an easy-going,

229

light-hearted sailor, always off to sea. He is to marry Jenifer who longingly awaits his return. However, when he does return it is only, he confesses, to get his share of the money that Gale has made through his, Pascoe's trading, so that he may marry another girl whom he has found over the sea. Gale has become a miser and when Pascoe begins to take his share of the gold, Gale murders him and throws his body into a pool. As Pascoe dies he declares that he will haunt Gale. Pascoe's ghost leads Gale to the pool and the terror-stricken Gale throws himself into the water and is drowned.

Maria Malibran	Robert Russell Bennett
	(1894-)

Première: New York, Juilliard Opera School, 1935, with alternating casts — Josephine Antoine and Helen Marshall as Maria, Allan Stewart and Arthur de Voss as Philip.
Romantic opera in three acts.
Book by Robert Simon.
Action: New York. 1825-1827.

The story deals with the American sojourn of the famous singer, Maria Malibran. Garcia, an operatic producer and father of Maria, a talented young singer, applies to the supposedly wealthy Malibran for financial aid. This is agreed upon with the understanding that Maria will be given him in marriage. Young Philip Cartwright is in love with Maria, but she gives him up in obedience to her father.

In time her marriage with Malibran is annulled. By this time she is a famous singer. Philip begs her to give up her art and marry him but she says it cannot be. A sad farewell between the two ends the story.

Garrick   Albert Stoessel
(1894-   )

Première: New York, Juilliard Opera School, 1937, with alternating casts—Pauline Pierce and Lucielle Browning as Peg, Donald Dickson and George Britton as David Garrick, Alice George and Maxine Stellman as Julia, Albert Gifford and Allen Stewart as Harry. Composer conducted.

Romantic opera in three acts. Libretto by Robert A. Simon, after the play, *David Garrick*.

Action: London, eighteenth century.

Peg Woffington, actress of Drury Lane Theatre, has quarrelled with her lover, David Garrick, and refuses to appear in his play. She has become jealous of his fascination for a beautiful face he has seen in the audience. Garrick's friend, Harry Marchmont, tells him that Julia, his beloved, has fallen in love with Garrick over the footlights. It develops that Julia and the beautiful face are the same. A duel at daybreak is the result. Garrick disarms Harry but nobly plays a part to disgust Julia and she rushes to the arms of Harry for protection. Peg and Garrick are reconciled and all ends well.

231

XXth CENTURY OPERA

American

The Man Without a Country	Walter Damrosch
	(1862-)

Première: New York, Metropolitan Opera House,
  1937, with Helen Traubel as Mary Rutledge,
  Arthur Carron as Philip Nolan, George Rasely as
  Harman Blennerhassett, Joseph Royer as Aaron
  Burr. Composer conducted.
Tragic opera in two acts. Libretto by Arthur Guiter-
  man.
Book adapted by the composer, from Edward Everett
  Hale's famous story, slightly changed for dramatic
  purposes by inserting more love interest.
Action: Blennerhassett Island in the Ohio River; Court-
  room Marine Barracks, Charleston, S. C. On board
  the *Guerriere* off Gibraltar, 1810-1815.

Blennerhassett is giving a party on his Ohio River estate,
at which Mary Rutledge and Philip Nolan, to whom she
is engaged, are present. Nolan is connected with Aaron
Burr's conspiracy to create an empire in the Southwest.
Mary warns Philip to have nothing to do with Burr, but
he is carried away with the idea of gaining riches which
he may bestow upon Mary, and he believes that Burr is a
great person. Burr and his confederates leave the island
as the United States authorities are on his trail. Philip remains because he has promised to see Mary again, and is
captured and charged with treason. During the court-
martial which follows, Philip damns the United States and
declares he never wants to hear of his country or see it
again. His sentence dooms him for lifelong exile aboard

232

ship. Mary determines to work for his pardon, knowing that the real offender has gone free. At Gibraltar the *Guerriere*, is at anchor and Mary comes on board to tell Philip that she has high hopes of his pardon, but he says he must win that for himself and that he wishes to give his life for his country as the only way that pardon can be won. A battle with sea robbers is pending and Commodore Decatur is to take command. He is Philip's classmate and consents to appoint Philip in charge of the cannon on the *Guerriere*. Philip is fatally wounded, and Decatur lays his own sword in Philip's arms as he lies dead on the deck.

The Captive   Gustave Strube
                                      (1867-   )

Première: Baltimore, 1938, by the Baltimore Civic
    Opera Company, with Margaret Gilner as Ra-
    mona, Brison Tucker as John Barton, Ada Gar-
    diner as Ormiston, Eugene Martinet as Portuguese
    Joe, Albert Wood as Pedro.
Tragic opera in three acts.
Book by Frederick A. Kummer.
Action: Port Royal, on the island of Jamaica, West
    Indies, close of seventeenth century.

Ramona, a lovely Spanish girl, has been captured by pirates and her father killed. She is made the slave and mistress of Ormiston, the leader of the pirates, and lives in misery and luxury, praying for death or for the strength

233

to kill her captor. Ormiston is absent on one of his raids and Ramona is insulted by Portuguese Joe, one of the pirates. John Barton, mate of a New England trading ship then in port, knocks the pirate down, and Joe swears revenge. Barton falls in love with Ramona, not knowing anything of her story, and she realizes that she loves him in turn. Portuguese Joe hides in the bushes and shoots Barton, who staggers into Ramona's garden. He is nursed back to life by Ramona and her maid with the aid of her faithful servant, Pedro. Ormiston returns and is killed by Pedro to save his beloved mistress. Barton, realizing that Ramona is Ormiston's mistress, denounces her for her deception and leaves the house. The pirates, believing that the Puritans have killed their chief, condemn the Puritans to be hung, but Ramona declares she has killed Ormiston and the Puritans are freed and driven away by the pirates. Ramona is to be hung for the crime, but Portuguese Joe has always desired her for himself and offers to buy her from his companions. This he does, but in the excitement, Pedro succeeds in giving her his knife and when Joe claims her as his property she defiantly declares that he shall have only her dead body. So he decides to sell her to the highest bidder. Barton has returned, his love being stronger than his Puritan training, and offers the highest price bid. However, Joe stabs Ramona and throws her, dying, into Barton's arms. Barton kneels with the dying girl in his arms and hears her with her last breath declare her love for him.

NOTE: The composer conducted, and the librettist, Frederick Kummer, was also present. They are both residents of Baltimore.

MEMORANDUM I
LIST OF COMPOSERS
WITH PRONUNCIATION, DATES
AND PAGE REFERENCES

LIST OF COMPOSERS
WITH PRONUNCIATION, DATES
AND PAGE REFERENCES

MEMORANDUM II
LIST OF OPERAS
WITH PAGE REFERENCES

LIST OF OPERAS
WITH PAGE REFERENCES

MEMORANDUM III
LIST OF OPERATIC STARS
WITH PAGE REFERENCES

LIST OF OPERATIC STARS
WITH PAGE REFERENCES